AMAZING & EXTRAORDINARY FACTS

CRICKET

AMAZING & EXTRAORDINARY FACTS

CRICKET

BRIAN LEVISON

CONTENTS

INTRODUCTION

Players know that there is rarely a cricket match where something doesn't happen worth talking about afterwards in the dressing room. If the incident is funny or unusual enough, it gets repeated in the pub, passed to the next team played, or it makes the local newspaper. Sometimes the many cricket trivia websites pick it up and it begins to develop a life of its own.

A good story is a good story, whether the episode took place on the village green or at Lord's, and the best have been included in this book. Gathered from across the cricketing world, they cover the period from the earliest days of recorded cricket in the mid-eighteenth century, right up to the present day. Here you will find false teeth, Jack the Ripper, the cycling cricketer, coconuts and the Worcester Cathedral clock. There are appearances by dominating personalities such as W.G. Grace and Sir Donald Bradman. You will also meet players whose cricketing impact was minimal, such as Frederick Hyland. His entire first-class career lasted for about five minutes, but his prominence in cricket lore is greater than many cricketers who played much longer (*see* Neither home nor away).

You may be surprised to learn that a Hollywood actor captained England (*see* From sightscreen to silver screen), or what happened when a Test debutant's wife looked away from the action for a split second (*see* The wife who came a purler). You will discover who didn't know of his selection as a *Wisden* Cricketer of the Year for 76 years (*see* Five of the best) and who began his first-class career at the age of 75 (*see* Golden oldies). A book like this can place otherwise forgotten names such as Jennings Tune (*see* Jennings Tune on song) or Victor Fuller-Eberle (*see* A costly drop) in the spotlight for a fleeting moment.

However unbelievable some of the stories may seem, they've been as thoroughly verified as far as checking allows, usually from two independent sources. This has meant adjusting one or two received versions. The Glamorgan bowler Peter Judge wasn't out bowled first ball in two innings within five minutes, although something like it did occur (*see* An out-and-out disaster). The immortal Ranjitsinhji didn't make three centuries in one day for three different teams, although two is a possibility. However he certainly made two first-class centuries for Sussex on the same day, glory enough. (*see* Jammy for the Jam Sahib).

And the stories keep coming. Just too late to make it into the book, *The Guardian* has reported that the umpires in a Lancashire v. Warwickshire game at Liverpool had to switch off the walkie-talkies they use to communicate with scorers because they were receiving messages from a local taxi firm.

I have had an enormous amount of assistance from Andrew Ward, Jill Haas, Derek Barnard, Matthew Levison and Jordan Urban, and take this opportunity to thank them very much for their time and help. Cricket must be one of the best-served sports for ease of accessing obscure information and the ability to find the scorecard of almost every game ever played on sites such as ESPN Cricinfo and CricketArchive was hugely helpful and time saving.

Abbreviations have been used to avoid tedious repetition of names in full and are listed at the back of the book, together with a short glossary of terms that may not be familiar to everyone.

The iron frame

How the Laws were changed to prevent cheating

These days the dimensions of bats, balls, stumps and probably the size of cap peaks are all carefully set out in the MCC Laws of Cricket. But this was not always the case. Up until the second half of the eighteenth century, the size of bats was not formalised. A bat could be as large as a player wished and could cover the wicket (22in by 6in/56cm by 15cm), theoretically providing the batsman with an unfair advantage. However it would have been unwieldy to use and wasn't thought to be a practical proposition. In any case, it was assumed no one would use such a bat because 'it wasn't cricket'.

In 1771 all that changed in 'a great cricket match' – as games of that era were always called – between the Hambledon and Chertsey clubs. A Chertsey player named White came in with a bat as wide, if not wider, than the wicket and used it very effectively. The Hambledon players were furious – not least because large stakes had been wagered – and they objected strongly. However White had broken no rules and could not be prevented from continuing to play, although ultimately his team lost the match by 1 run.

Afterwards, the Hambledon players made a formal protest and the rules were changed to make the maximum width of a bat 4.25in (11cm) – this ruling has remained in place ever since. The Hambledon Club – the world's first cricket club and the MCC of its day – implemented this rule very strictly. The Club constructed an iron frame of the correct width; each bat was tested, and any exceeding the dimensions were sternly rejected.

Very occasionally a batsman is still found to have an over-wide bat. In 1991, when Keith Arthurton was playing for the West Indies Board of Control XI against Australia in Bridgetown, Barbados, the Australian player Dean Jones spotted that Arthurton's bat looked a little on the large side. It was measured and found to be 4.5in (11.5cm) wide although Arthurton was allowed to continue using it.

As well as ultra-wide bats, bowlers

had another problem to contend with. Wickets in the early days of the game had only two stumps with a bail across the top. For a batsman to be out bowled the bail had to be dislodged, which could only happen if the stumps were hit. However a ball could, and sometimes did, pass directly through the centre of the wicket without dislodging the bail.

When this happened several times in an important match between Hambledon Club and All England in 1775, the rules were changed and a third stump was introduced. Even so, in the 1997–98 Test series between Pakistan and South Africa, Pat Symcox of South Africa was bowled off stump by Mushtaq Ahmed, yet the bail stayed in place due to faulty manufacture.

Over 200 years after the third stump rule change, the Australian Dennis Lillee, one of the great fast bowlers, outwitted the Laws. In the first innings of the Australia v. England Test match in 1979 at Perth, Australia, he came to the wicket with an aluminium bat called the 'ComBat' that had been made by a friend's company. Strictly, this bat was not against the Laws, which omitted to state that bats should be made of only wood. Lillee had in fact used a similar bat in a Test match against the West Indies a few days earlier without complaint.

The captains of both teams objected to the bat, although for different reasons. The Australian captain, Greg Chappell, thought a shot by Lillee for three would have gone for four with a wooden bat; the England captain, Mike Brearley, said the metal bat was damaging the ball and putting his bowlers at a disadvantage. Chappell's opposition was half genuine, half pretence.

He had seen Lillee practising the day before and knew he intended to use the ComBat. He reckoned that annoying his ace fast bowler would fire him up to bowl that much more aggressively.

The umpires told Lillee to change his bat but he refused. The game was held up for ten minutes while Lillee, the captains and the umpires discussed the rights and wrongs. Eventually Lillee was disgruntledly persuaded to use a wooden bat. The publicity sent aluminium bat sales soaring until the Laws were amended to outlaw it.

ON YER BIKE!

If a cricketer has displeased his captain through a piece of poor fielding, or if the captain is simply not concentrating, a fielder can find himself at long leg for one over and at third man for the next, two fielding positions about as far apart as they can be, at a distance of 120yds (110m) or more. On one occasion the Essex cricketer Keith Pont, finding himself fielding in these positions and wishing to save his legs, borrowed a spectator's bicycle and pedalled his way to the other side of the ground.

Waugh of words

Witty retorts under pressure

It is not always obvious to spectators but a fair amount of backchat goes on between the batsmen and fielders. When this is aimed at distracting the batsman or bowler, it is a form of gamesmanship known as sledging. Sledging is most often the attempt by the fielding side to break the batsman's concentration, although it can work the other way around. The best sledging is notable for quick-witted responses under pressure. Here are some classic examples that, like many good stories, turn up in different versions.

The Australian batsman Mark Waugh played in 128 Tests with

a batting average of over 40, an impressive record. Even so, it was inferior to that of his twin brother, Steve, who played more Tests, had an average of over 50, and captained Australia through an outstandingly successful period. In one Test, when the fringe England player James Ormond came to the crease, Mark gave him an aggressive welcome: 'Mate, what are you doing here? There's no way you're good enough to play for England!' 'Maybe not,' replied Ormond, 'but at least I'm the best player in my family!'

Playing for Glamorgan against Somerset, the fast bowler Greg Thomas managed to beat the West Indies master batsman Viv Richards for pace a few balls in a row. Ill-advisedly he informed Richards 'It's red, round and weighs about 5 ounces, in case you were wondering.' The very next delivery, Richards hit him for six and retorted, 'Greg, you know what it looks like. Now go and fetch it!'

W.G. Grace was such a commanding figure in cricket that he was able to dominate umpires and players. Once, after being given out lbw, he refused to walk off, saying to the bowler 'The crowd has come to watch me bat, not you bowl.' On another occasion, after appeals for lbw and a catch behind the wicket were given not out in successive balls, the bowler Charles Kortright felt Grace was intimidating the umpire. Kortright was reportedly the fastest bowler of his time and his next ball to Grace was an express delivery that knocked two of Grace's stumps out of the ground. As Grace passed him on the way back to the pavilion, Kortright remarked sardonically 'Surely you're not going, doctor?

There's still one stump standing!'

In a Test match between Zimbabwe and Australia, the Australian fast bowler Glenn McGrath was bowling to the chunky Zimbabwe number 11, Eddo Brandes. When he failed to get Brandes out as quickly as he expected, McGrath demanded brusquely 'Why are you so fat?' Brandes may not have been much good as a batsman but his riposte made even the Australian fielders laugh: 'Because every time I make love to your wife, she gives me a biscuit.'

Sometimes a player can be sledged by his own teammate. In 1993, England was playing India at the Wankhede Stadium. Prior to the game, an England pace bowler told Robin Smith that he could get the Indian batsman Vinod Kambli out with an orange. When Kambli reached 200, Smith remarked to him 'Don't you think it's time you pulled out that bloody orange?'

Spectators like to join in the fun, too. The England spinner Phil Tufnell, a fine bowler but not the best of fielders, was once barracked while fielding in Australia: 'Hey Tufnell, lend me your brains, I'm building an idiot!' Another Aussie spectator once shouted at an English batsman taking time out to adjust his protective box: 'They're the only balls you've touched all day!'

'Prophetic' sledging occurred on the MCC's 1950-51 tour of Australia. As reported by the former Australian Test captain Ian Chappell, when the England fast bowler John Warr got off the boat someone shouted at him 'Hey Warr, you've got as much chance of taking a Test wicket on this tour as I have of pushing a pound of butter up a parrot's arse with a hot needle!' This would have turned out to be true if the Australian spin bowler Ian Johnson hadn't taken pity on Warr and 'walked' for a non-existent catch to give him a solitary wicket. After the first two Tests, Warr never played for England again and his Test bowling average of 281 is the worst of any England player.

Over-dressed for the occasion

Sid Barnes takes the mickey

The 12th man is a general dogsbody. He has to be ready to dash on at short notice to field as substitute, bring out a replacement bat or gloves and – most importantly – hand out the drinks during the breaks. It's a job no one really wants, so it was a surprise when the Australian Test batsman Sid Barnes offered to be 12th man for New South Wales in their Sheffield Shield match against South Australia at the Adelaide Oval in 1952.

Being 12th man also implies that you are not good enough to be in the first team. This certainly wasn't the case with Barnes. He had scored 152 for NSW in the previous game and had been a member of Don Bradman's Invincibles side on their 1948 tour of England. It could have been that he wanted to give a younger player a chance. However his behaviour suggests it might have been pique at failing to be selected for the Australian Test team, possibly by annoying the selectors with his erratic behaviour.

His actions on the second day of the match effectively ended any chances he ever had of playing for Australia again. During a drinks interval he appeared on the ground looking more like Jeeves than a cricketer. Very dapper in a double-breasted suit and tie (rather than his cricketing whites) and sporting a red carnation in his buttonhole, he was accompanied by a steward carrying two panniers covered with a cloth to protect their contents from the sun. In the baskets were items such as cigars, iced towels, a scent spray, a portable radio, a mirror and a clothes brush. The incident started off as a joke but the interval became protracted and the crowd stopped seeing the funny side.

Apologies were demanded which Barnes refused to give. Eventually his state cricket association wrote one for him. After that, Barnes played only once more for NSW. He died aged 57, a suspected suicide. His waspish sense of humour is illustrated by an incident on the tour of England in 1948. The umpire Alec Skelding had just turned down a strong Australian appeal and at that moment a dog ran on to the field. Barnes captured it and passed it to Skelding with the comment 'Now all you want is a white stick.'

From sightscreen to silver screen

Cricket takes to the stage

Strong links between cricket and the stage date back to the 1890s and the heyday of the hugely popular English comedian Dan Leno. Leno organised slapstick cricket matches at venues such as Stamford Bridge and the Oval. The crowds loved them and attended in large numbers, raising good sums of money for charity.

Boldly, in February 1908, an attempt was made to take cricket into the theatre itself. This project was the brainchild of the theatre manager Oswald Stoll, the impresario who ran the London Coliseum. In his book entitled *The House that Stoll Built*, author Frederick Muller tells how Stoll loved to present large-scale entertainments such as chariot racing set in the context of the early Christians battling Roman gladiators, nymphs diving into a large glass tank or torchlight tattoos.

In this vein of entertainment, Stoll organised a four-a-side game between Surrey and Middlesex to take place in his theatre every

evening for a week. Some well-known cricketers such as Albert Trott (*see* The bowler who bowled too well) and Jack Hearne were playing, although many of the best Surrey players, including Jack Hobbs, were on tour overseas. The rules were very approximate. The pitch was 15yds (14m) long and it was hit-and-run. The official scorer was on stage, although if the ball disappeared into the wings it was this person's job to retrieve it. The audience were given cards for keeping score and were protected from contact with fierce hooks or cover drives by an auditorium net.

Daily information about the game's progress appeared on a bulletin board outside the theatre. Stoll made sure the tension was maintained until the last night of the show when Middlesex beat Surrey and were presented with a cheap tankard as a trophy; the players were paid £5 for their efforts. The venture does not seem to have been repeated and the only cricket seen in the theatre since then has been in plays such as *Outside Edge* by Richard Harris and Richard Bean's *The English Game*, which were almost as good as the real thing.

Someone who was the real thing in both theatrical and cricketing terms was the actor C. Aubrey Smith (1863-1948). He played 143 first-class games for Sussex and other teams, and was known as 'Round-the-Corner Smith' because of his peculiar run up. He was good enough to play for England in South Africa in 1889 when he captained the team in the first Test. Injured, he dropped out of the second Test and never played for England again.

Later he moved to Hollywood where he appeared in a diverse range of films with stars such as Clark Gable, Laurence Olivier, Maurice Chevalier and Gary Cooper and even, right at the end of his career, Elizabeth Taylor. He founded the Hollywood Cricket Club and insisted all the British stars like David Niven, Boris Karloff and Leslie Howard play for him. Under his influence, they probably took it a lot more seriously than Dan Leno and his players.

A NOVEL TYPE OF SUNSHADE

At 6ft 3in (1.9m) tall and weighing 21st (133kg) Warwick Armstrong, captain of Australia on their successful 1921 Ashes tour of England, was nicknamed 'The Big Ship'. His outsize shirt and shoes are still fondly exhibited in the Australian Cricket Hall of Fame. On one occasion, while inspecting a wicket after a rain break during a Test match, he was advised by a spectator to 'Roll on it! Roll on it!' as a method of drying the wicket.

During a tour match at Southampton, Armstrong was ambling around the perimeter on a hot day watching two of his team making centuries, when he noticed a young boy was following him. Thinking that the lad wanted his autograph, but was too shy to ask, Armstrong said 'Here give me your autograph book and I'll sign it.' The boy said he hadn't got one. 'Then what do you want?' Armstrong asked. 'Please, sir,' the boy is said to have replied, 'you are the only bit of decent shade in the place.'

Armstrong didn't mind telling a story against himself and relates how he was once batting with the Australian bowler Arthur Mailey. As Mailey was taking guard, he shouted up the pitch to Armstrong asking him to move. 'What, can't you see the bowler?' Armstrong asked. 'See the bowler?' Mailey replied, 'I can't see the * sightscreen!'***

12 o'clock and all's Wells

How Bomber beat the clock

Bryan 'Bomber' Wells, an off-spin bowler who played for Gloucestershire and Nottinghamshire from 1951 to 1965, did not look much like a first-class cricketer. He was not the slimmest of men, he trundled in to bowl off a run up no longer than a pace or two, his fielding displayed a lack of urgency that would have disqualified him from the modern game, and his lifetime batting average of 7.47 says all you need to know about that side of his talents. Perhaps ironically, Wells called himself 'Bomber' after the British heavyweight boxer 'Bombardier' Billy Wells, who beat the gong at the start of Rank Organisation films.

Although he looked innocuous as a bowler, Wells had a highly successful career. Towards the end of his last season, when someone told him he had taken 999 first-class wickets, he decided to retire straight away. Naturally, he was asked why he didn't wait until he had taken his 1,000th. He replied that he'd be remembered more for retiring on 999 than for

taking 1,000. Very soon after he retired, it was discovered that in fact he'd only taken 998.

Wells took his cricket seriously but thought it should also be fun. On one occasion, he was preparing to bowl at Worcester when he saw that the nearby cathedral clock was about to strike midday. He quickly arranged with the batsman, Roly Jenkins, to try and bowl an over before the clock had finished chiming; Jenkins duly patted each delivery back to him. Half a minute later the over was finished and the clock was still chiming. His captain, Sir Derrick Bailey, accused Wells of making a mockery of the game and told him that he must take a longer run. So Wells went back 8 or 9yds (7 or 8m), took his normal run of a couple of paces and bowled from 25 or 26yds (23 or 24m). It is said that the ball still finished on a length. However his captain wasn't impressed and dropped him for the next two games.

On another occasion, he was bowling to a young batsman who kept stepping away just as Wells was about to deliver. For his next attempt, the exasperated Wells did a complete tour of the square, past all the fielders on the leg side, behind the wicket-keeper and then up the off side all the way back to his bowling position. 'Are you ready now?' he shouted at the batsman, and bowled him first ball.

The hunt for the missing run

How a world record almost wasn't

One of the most famous records in cricket is the 555 put on by the Yorkshiremen Percy Holmes and Herbert Sutcliffe in the Essex v. Yorkshire game at Leyton in 1932. At the time it was the highest ever first wicket partnership and is still the highest partnership for any wicket in English cricket and the seventh highest for any wicket in the world.

The previous record was 554 by Jack Brown and John Tunnicliffe, also Yorkshiremen, set in 1898. As soon as they had made the new one, Holmes and Sutcliffe shook hands mid-pitch in a rare display of emotion. Job done, Sutcliffe took a wild swing at the next ball and was out. Yorkshire declared and the pair posed under the scoreboard. But even as they prepared for a photograph, the total on the board moved back to 554. The scorers had re-counted and the record hadn't been beaten after all. There was consternation, especially among the many Yorkshire supporters who had travelled down overnight to be present at the historic occasion.

All eyes fixed unbelievingly on the scoreboard. Then it suddenly moved back to 555. General sighs of relief; Sutcliffe and Holmes were famously photographed. But what had happened? According to the journalist and broadcaster Alan Gibson, then aged nine and present at the game, scoring in those days could be a trifle 'haphazard'. From time to time one of the scorers would take a break and wander around the ground. He would update his scorebook on his return by copying from the book of his colleague, who would then himself have a break. In those circumstances it is easy to see how a run or two could go astray.

According to the Essex captain Charlie Bray, the discrepancy arose for a different reason. He said that the Essex scorer had not been at his seat for the first ball of the day.

A no-ball had been called but had gone unrecorded in his book. Later the umpire confirmed he had called a no-ball and the Essex scorer agreed to enter it in his book, and the record was confirmed. Subsequent research has not proved the point either way. Yet another story says the matter was resolved when a parson who had been keeping score came up with his scorebook and confirmed the record. The demoralised Essex side lost the game by an innings and 313 runs. The record stood until beaten in 1977 in a game held in Karachi.

From ashes to The Ashes

Origins of cricket's most famous rivalry

The most celebrated obituary in cricket does not chronicle the life and death of a cricket legend but instead a rather unexpected jolt to English national honour. In 1882, five years after the first Test match between England and Australia in Australia, the colonials had the temerity to beat England ***on** English soil* for the first time ever. So stunned was the English cricketing public at

CONTAINING THE 'ASHES' OF ENGLISH CRICKET: AN URN IN THE POSSESSION OF LORD DARNLEY.

this reversal of the natural order that a satirical obituary appeared in *The Sporting Times*. It proclaimed that English cricket had died and that 'the body will be cremated and the ashes taken to Australia'.

When the time came for the next Test series – this time in Australia – the newspapers picked up on the ashes image, stating that the English side was going to Australia to try and regain 'the Ashes'. Thus was born the sobriquet for all future Test matches between the two countries, and the term has come to represent probably the fiercest and most widely followed contest in international cricket.

The Ashes is played in England

and Australia alternately, usually with five Test matches per series. If neither country wins the series outright then the one already holding The Ashes retains them.

But do real ashes exist and if so, where? During England's 1882-83 tour of Australia, a group of Melbourne women presented Ivo Bligh, the England captain, with a small terracotta urn only 4in (11cm) high understood to contain the ashes of a bail. There are two labels on the urn; the first inscribed 'The Ashes' and the second containing six lines of not very deathless verse.

Although Bligh treated the urn as a personal gift, after his death in 1927 his widow presented it to the MCC who placed it in the Lord's Museum. Because of its fragility it remains there permanently, regardless of which country wins a series, although it has left the museum on three occasions, most recently on a trip to Australia in 2006. It was not the only Ashes memorial to be created but it has outlasted all others and is the one everyone thinks of as The Ashes. Up until the 1998-99 series, the Ashes holder had to be content with the glory alone, but from then forwards the winner has received a crystal representation of the famous urn.

The only blemish

Don Bradman and the 1948 Invincibles

It is generally acknowledged that the greatest of all sides to tour England were the 1948 Australians, captained by the legendary Don Bradman. Their touring party also included other cricket immortals such as Keith Miller, Ray Lindwall, Neil Harvey, Don Tallon and Sid Barnes. The Australians' tour record was outstanding: they played 31 first-class games, winning 23 and drawing the rest, the first side to remain unbeaten throughout a tour of England.

On the first day of a match against Essex they scored 721, the highest total ever achieved in a single day. During his innings of 187, Bradman hit the first three balls of one over to the cover-point boundary. The Essex wicket-keeper facetiously asked him 'Can't you hit them anywhere else?' The Don hit the next three balls pitched in exactly the same spot

to the mid-wicket boundary. Essex still managed to draw some wry satisfaction from the fact that '... We were the only county to get the Australians all out in a day during the summer.' In other games the Australians scored 774 and twice scored over 600. They won the five-match Test series 4-0. Unsurprisingly, the team is known to cricketing history as The Invincibles.

If there was a tiny blemish in the tour record it came in the fifth Test, Bradman's last. The match situation was such that he would probably bat just once and needed to score only 4 runs to achieve the amazing batting average of 100 in Test cricket (no one else has exceeded 66). After receiving three cheers from the England team, he played the first ball from Eric Hollies confidently enough, but was bowled second ball for a duck by a googly. He had to be content with a Test average of a mere 99.94 to go with his lifetime batting average of 95.14.

A QUACKING GOOD STORY

In the believe-it-or-not department of cricket stories that might just be true is one involving Walt Disney and Don Bradman. In 1932 Bradman and the Australians were on an intense tour of North America, playing 51 matches in 76 days. The already famous Bradman had recently married and, like many cricketers, was spending his honeymoon on the cricket field. He scored heavily against poor sides in New York, Toronto and Vancouver. However his all-conquering progress came to a halt on 16 July, playing against the New York West Indians: he was out

for a duck c. Olivierre b. Clarke.

Apparently this news created such a sensation that it made the US newspapers, and even Walt Disney heard about it. He was so enchanted by the idea that the great Bradman had failed that he decided to name a new character his studio was developing after the cricketer. And that – perhaps – is how Donald Duck got his name.

It is certainly possible that Disney saw the Australians play in Hollywood in August 1932. The timeline also fits: the first Donald Duck cartoon was not released until June 1934. On the other hand, there is a reference to a duck in Disney's cartoon plans as early as 1931, although whether the character had a name is not clear. Likely or not, what can one say but Jiminy Cricket?

0, 0, 0*, 1, 1*, 0, 0, 0, 0, 1*, 0, 0, 0, 0
The worst batsman in the world

The winner of this unwanted title depends on how you define 'worst'. Is it the fewest runs, the lowest average, appearing not to know which end of the bat to hold, or the unfailing ability to fulfil everyone's lowest expectations?

A pre-eminent candidate for the title is New Zealand's Chris Martin. In his first 94 innings in Test matches, he scored only 112 runs. In half of them he was not out, so his Test average works out at 2.38 with a highest score of 12 not out. The Zimbabwe fast bowler Pommie Mbangwa achieved an even lower average in Test cricket of 2. However he had a first-class average of 6.89 so can be considered quite competent.

If you're willing to consider the

judgement of a horse in this, you may be interested in Fred Morley, the old England and Nottinghamshire fast bowler who played from 1871 to 1883. As soon as Morley came into bat Horace, the horse that rolled the Trent Bridge pitch between innings, would amble slowly towards the roller and allow himself to be hitched up. Morley had a lifetime batting average of 5, so Horace was rarely wrong.

Eric Hollies, the old England and Warwickshire leg spinner, and the man who had the distinction of bowling Bradman for a duck in his last Test innings, took more wickets (2,323) than he scored runs (1,673) at an average of 5. He also held the world record of 71 consecutive innings without reaching double figures. However, he must be credited with saving a Test match against South Africa with an innings of 18 not out, so perhaps this disqualifies him?

In 1907, the Yorkshire fast bowler George Deyes had the sequence of 14 innings which looks more like binary code than someone's scores: 0, 0, 0*, 1, 1*, 0, 0, 0, 0, 1*, 0, 0, 0, 0. Amongst modern players Ed Giddins, Alan Mullally, Peter Such and Phil Tufnell have strong claims for inclusion, but it is hard to look beyond Mark Robinson, a fast-medium bowler who played for Northamptonshire, Yorkshire and Sussex from 1987 to 2002. In 259 career innings he scored 590 runs at an average of about 4; however he did have purple patches of badness. In 1989 he scored 17 runs from 23 innings at an average of only 1.30, even allowing for ten not outs. In 1990 he did even better (or worse), scoring only 3 runs the entire season. From 15 May to 18 August, he set a world record by failing to score in 12 consecutive innings, although seven were not out. At one stage in his career he played 61 consecutive innings without reaching double figures, behind only Eric Hollies' 71 and Nobby Clark's 65.

AN OUT-AND-OUT BATTING DISASTER

For batsmen who fail to score, cricket has invented expressions like ducks, golden ducks, pairs and king pairs. Yet there should be special terminology for what happened to Peter Judge, a good bowler but not much of a batsman. Playing for Glamorgan against the Indians at Cardiff in 1946, Peter was last man in and was bowled by Sarwate for a golden duck. Glamorgan were over 200 runs behind and were asked to follow on.

It happened that the not-out batsman at the other end was the Glamorgan captain J.C. Clay. With only 25 overs left, Clay knew there was virtually no chance that his team would lose the game. So in order that the crowd would see as much cricket as possible, he waived the ten-minute break between innings, and to save time decided that he and Judge would stay out on the pitch and open the batting. Judge prepared to face Sarwate again. Within a couple of deliveries he was out; again bowled, again without scoring.

Although it makes a better story to say that he was once more out first ball, as is usually reported, the Glamorgan scorebook shows it was second ball. What is indisputable is that he was out clean bowled twice in three balls within a minute or so, a unique occurrence. Glamorgan came close to losing the match but Judge's experience deserves its own nomenclature. An out-and-out disaster, perhaps?

Jennings Tune on song
Ultimate bowling performances

For a bowler to take all ten wickets in an innings without conceding a run seems, at first sight, about as likely as a monkey producing the works of Shakespeare given a durable enough keyboard and sufficient time. But in fact there are 24 recorded instances of such a cricketing feat – although none at first-class level.

So, possibly the bar should be raised a little higher. What about the extreme perfection of taking ten for none with all ten wickets clean bowled? Perhaps surprisingly, this has happened at least twice. The first occasion was in Yorkshire by Jennings Tune for Cliffe when they played Eastrington in 1922. In more recent memory Alex Kelly, aged 17, did so in 1994 playing for Bishop Auckland against Newton Aycliffe in a 20-over evening match of the Milburngate Durham County Junior League.

Bishop Auckland batted first and scored 150 for one. Alex came on to bowl with the opposition at 36 for none. Having been demoted from one to four in the batting order, he had not had a bat and was apparently feeling a little peeved. Perhaps motivated by his annoyance, he took two wickets in his first three balls, three in the second over, two in the third, two in the fourth and the final wicket off the third ball of his fifth over. Newton Aycliffe were all out for 47 and Alex had taken all ten wickets clean bowled in 27 balls.

In the world of first-class cricket,

taking all ten wickets in an innings clean bowled has been achieved only once, in 1850 at Lord's in the South v. North game. The bowler, playing for the North and bowling roundarm, was one of the great names of cricket. To find out who, *see* Cricket's greatest name?

An unfortunate bowler once took nine wickets in nine balls, and then got taken off. In a school game in Blenheim, New Zealand, in 1967 Stephen Fleming took the last wicket of Bohally Intermediate School's first innings against Marlborough College 'A'. In the second innings he opened the bowling – they were eight-ball overs – and took another eight wickets in eight balls. He then got taken off in favour of a boy who had taken a hat trick in the first innings. For the record, Bohally were all out for three in 21 balls.

Having started by comparing the likelihood of ten wicket hauls for no runs to monkeys typing Shakespeare, it is worth mentioning that in 2011 the *Daily Mail* reported that a team of virtual monkeys had been set to work at computers and produced 99.9 per cent of Shakespeare's oeuvre.

When underarm was underhand

It was legal – but was it fair?

The grandiosely named 1980-81 Benson & Hedges World Series Cup between Australia, New Zealand and India took place at various grounds around Australia. It was one of those interminable one-day triangular series where each side plays the other two innumerable times in order to eliminate one of them. Then the two remaining sides play four more matches to decide a winner.

This series, like so many before and since, would have been instantly forgettable except for one of the most controversial incidents in modern cricket. The third of the

finals took place on 1 February 1981 at Melbourne Cricket Ground. Each side had won one game, so the situation was tense in terms of the overall series. As the last over began, the match was also delicately poised. Australia looked better placed, as New Zealand needed to score 15 to win. After five deliveries, they still needed 7. They could tie the game by hitting a six off the last ball but, assuming there was no wide or no-ball, could not win it. Still, a tie would keep the series even.

Determined not to give New Zealand the slightest chance, the hard-nosed Australian captain Greg Chappell took a very unusual – and some would say unsporting – course of action. He instructed the bowler, his younger brother Trevor, to underarm the last ball along the ground. The umpire and the batsman were informed. Everyone was taken aback: underarm had effectively gone out in the nineteenth century. As soon as he realised what was going on Rod Marsh, the Australian wicket-keeper, indicated 'No mate, don't do it.' Up in the commentary box Ian Chappell, Greg's older brother and a former Australian captain, is reported to have called out 'No, Greg, no, you can't do that!' The New Zealand lower-order batsman Brian McKechnie, having first dropped his bat in surprise, could do nothing with the delivery and Australia won the game by 6 runs. The home crowd was disgusted and booed the Australians off the field.

Unsurprisingly there was a good deal of post-match reaction. What Greg Chappell had done was legal, but was it in the spirit of the game? The Prime Ministers of both countries became involved: Robert Muldoon of New Zealand called it 'an act of true cowardice', while Malcolm Fraser of Australia said it was 'contrary to the traditions of the game.' The general reaction was, to use the highest term of disapproval, 'it's not cricket'.

One of the Australian team, Doug Walters, slightly wondered what all the fuss was about. 'Why didn't he hit the ball for six?' he asked Allan Border, who replied, as we all would have, 'Because it was rolling along the ground.' The next day Walters took Border out on to the pitch and instructed him to underarm a ball.

Walters stuck out his left boot, the ball cannoned off it into the air and Walters swiped it for six. Why hadn't McKechnie done that? However, it has to be said that if McKechnie had had the presence of mind to do that, the chances are that he would have been given out 'hit the ball twice'.

The authorities raised their eyebrows but took no action against Greg Chappell. However they showed what they thought of his behaviour by subsequently outlawing the underarm delivery as 'not within the spirit of the game' unless both captains agree in advance it can be used. The only player who received a 'wigging' was McKechnie. He was censured because he had thrown his bat on the ground in disgust after the ball had been bowled. In the long term the Chappells suffered lasting damage to their cricketing reputations, the incident being the first thing that comes to mind when their names are mentioned.

BEETROOT WITH MUSTARD AND ONIONS ON THE SIDE

George Beet was the Derbyshire wicket-keeper from 1910 to 1925. He often used to take catches off the bowler Fred Root, so the appearance of c. Beet b. Root on the score sheet caused as much delight then as the Durham combination of c. Mustard b. Onions does to us today.

In February 1981, the South African-born English Test player Allan Lamb was batting for Western Province against a Transvaal team that included Jimmy Cook and Clive Rice. He reached 130 before he was out Lamb c. Cook b. Rice (Lamb

caught Cook boiled Rice?). Transvaal had Cook, Rice and Pollock (a species of fish) batting at two, three and four – almost a complete menu.

Furthermore, back in 1878 England had Wyld batting at six and Flowers at seven, a fragrant partnership if ever there was one.

Collecting bug

The world's most expensive cricket book

Depending on how you define 'book', it is estimated that there are some 30,000 of them on the subject of cricket. As you might expect, the largest public collection is thought to be in the Lord's library – this totals about 11,000 volumes. Here they have rare gems such as the only manuscript copy of W.G. Grace's *Cricket*, and the only complete set of Britcher's *Scores*. Britcher, probably the MCC's first official scorer, published an annual set of scorecards from 1790 to 1805, the first person to do so in an organised way. He was to pave the way for *Wisden Cricketers' Almanack* 60 years later,

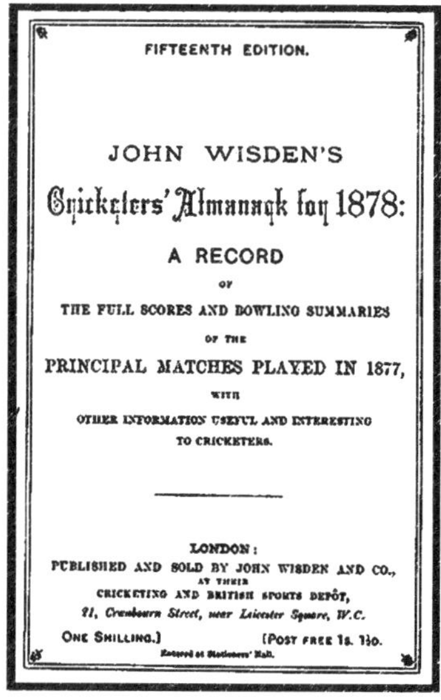
FIFTEENTH EDITION.

JOHN WISDEN'S

Cricketers' Almanack for 1878:

A RECORD

OF

THE FULL SCORES AND BOWLING SUMMARIES

OF THE

PRINCIPAL MATCHES PLAYED IN 1877,

WITH

OTHER INFORMATION USEFUL AND INTERESTING TO CRICKETERS.

LONDON:

PUBLISHED AND SOLD BY JOHN WISDEN AND CO.,

AT THEIR

CRICKETING AND BRITISH SPORTS DEPÔT,

21, Cranbourn Street, near Leicester Square, W.C.

ONE SHILLING.] [POST FREE 1s. 1½d.

Entered at Stationers' Hall.

universally regarded as cricket's bible.

Yet there is at least one collection that is larger than Lord's. For many years Geoffrey Coppinger's 16,000 volumes was the largest and when he died it was purchased by Tim Bunting to add to his own. It is believed that Bunting now has over 25,000 volumes housed in a purpose-built library, and that his is the largest collection in the world. His prize possessions include two complete runs of *Wisden*, with yet another set that is truly unique and enviable: W.G. Grace's own personal signed set, which Bunting bought for £150,000.

Cricket lovers are among the most avid collectors of cricketing memorabilia, particularly books. They will spend thousands of pounds trying to collect a complete set of *Wisden*, knowing that the early volumes from 1864 virtually never appear on the market. They have to be content with filling the gaps in their run with the facsimile copies that have become available in recent years. Other cricket memorabilia are also valuable: the baggy green cap worn by Bradman in his final Test once sold for £184,000 and a Sachin Tendulkar record-breaking bat sold for £59,000.

The record price for a cricket book was paid for *Cricket: A Collection of All the Grand Matches of Cricket Played in England from 1771 to 1791*, written by William Epps. This book of about 100 pages fills in details of matches not included in Britcher's Scores and is so rare that not even the British Library has a copy. It is believed that the MCC held two copies, and it was one of these that was sold at Christie's in November 2010 when an unnamed buyer paid the staggering figure of £151,250, a world record price for a cricket book. In the same sale one volume of Britcher's *Scores* was sold for £55,250, quite a good amount for a 30-page pamphlet of largely unknown teams and cricketers – unless you've caught the collecting bug.

CRICKET, THE IRISH QUESTION AND A DILEMMA

As one of the nineteenth-century's most prominent nationalists discovered, dedication to a political cause can conflict with a love of cricket. In 1880, a team of English cricketers based in New York and other US locations was due to play a US team in Philadelphia. At the last moment, one of the team called off and the English side looked around for a replacement. An Irish member of the team recalled that Charles Stewart Parnell, the passionate leader of the Irish Home Rule movement, was then in New York raising funds for Irish famine relief. Parnell was a very keen cricketer and the captain of a County Wicklow team. He came

from a cricket-mad family: in 1859, when Parnell was only 13, his father had defied doctor's orders to play in a cricket match and had died the following day.

The Irishman had often played against Parnell in Ireland and felt sure he would be interested in making up the numbers. Together, he and a companion set off for Parnell's hotel. They went up to his room where they found him in bed and explained the situation. Parnell was immediately attracted by the idea. 'Who is the match between?' he asked as he started to get out of bed. 'It's England v. America,' his acquaintance said. 'Oh...' Parnell replied thoughtfully, 'England v. America. I am afraid that won't quite do. It won't do. It will get into the papers and if I'm playing on a side entitled "England" they'll kick up no end of a row at home.' In the event, the game was 'played on a soggy turf' and ended in a draw after time was lost to bad weather, so perhaps Parnell did not miss too much in the way of enjoyable cricket.

A costly drop

The 600-run gift

To have your death recorded in *Wisden* implies the achievement of great cricketing deeds. Yet the two-line entry in the 1975 *Wisden* recording the passing of Victor Fuller-Eberle, aged 87, shows that his sole claim to fame was an easy catch he dropped, at the age of 11, when playing in a school game at Clifton College, Bristol.

The occasion was a junior house match between Clark's House and North Town. This took place over the course of four afternoons in June 1899 – such matches were 'timeless' – and Clark's House won by the convincing margin of an innings and

688 runs. In the context of North Town's batting performance – all out for 87 in the first innings and for 61 in the second – Fuller-Eberle's 8 in the first innings and top score of 15 in the second were not bad efforts, considering he was the youngest player on the field. He was obviously no sporting duffer: as a rugby player, he was later good enough to have a trial for England.

However it is true that the dropped catch was probably a decisive blow against his team, as the man he missed was the captain of the opposing team, A.E.J. Collins. Collins, aged 13, was on 20 but went on to make 628 not out, still the highest individual score ever recorded. Collins was dropped on three or four other occasions but only Fuller-Eberle's missed chance earned an obituary in *Wisden*.

As Collins' innings developed, the news spread and a large crowd began to follow the match, ignoring the other games in progress; even *The Times* reported on it. Collins hit one six, four fives, 31 fours, 33 threes,

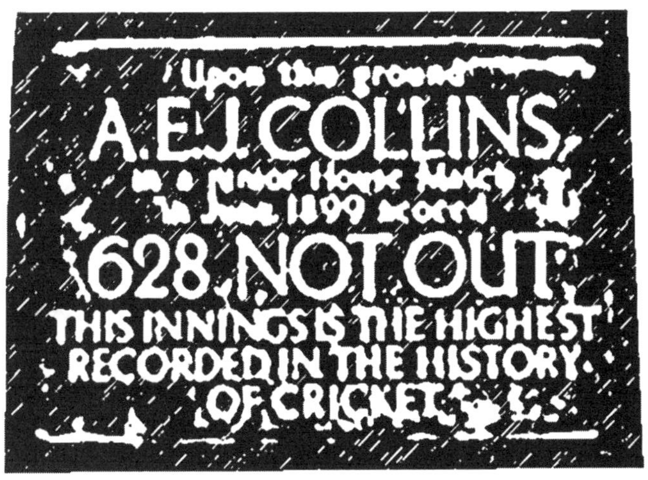

146 twos and 87 singles. Among the milestones he passed was the then world record score of 485 by Andrew Stoddart. As Collins also took seven wickets in North Town's first innings and four in the second, he had a good game and might well have won the Man of the Match had it then existed. The scorecard hangs in the cricket pavilion at Clifton College although even the scorers could not say for sure how many runs Collins had made.

After he left school, Collins joined the Army. He never played first-class cricket although he did play at Lord's, scoring 58 and 36 for the Royal Engineers against the Royal Artillery. He was killed in action in 1914 at the first battle of Ypres, aged 29. He never liked to be reminded of the famous innings that gave him and Fuller-Eberle cricketing immortality.

The Blackheath number four

The cricketer linked to five unsolved murders

What could be the possible connection between the 1888 Jack the Ripper murders of five young women and the Blackheath Cricket Club? One answer is none; another, a thin tissue of coincidences that tenuously linked the Blackheath number four of that period,

Montague Druitt, to one of the greatest unsolved murder mysteries of the nineteenth century.

The first coincidence occurred on 8 September 1888, the day the body of the second of the murdered women, Annie Chapman, was found dead with her throat slashed. The same day Blackheath was playing the Christopherson family team (*see* All in the family) and beat them by 22 runs. The second coincidence is that the Ripper murders ceased very close to the time, probably early December, that Druitt allegedly committed suicide.

Montague Druitt was a not-particularly-well off barrister who became a part-time teacher in 1880 to supplement his income. Outside work, cricket was his great passion. He was a good bowler who never played first-class cricket but batted and bowled well enough to play for Dorset and at a good standard of club cricket. He played with and against well-known players such as Lord Harris, Bobby Abel and Stanley Christopherson (the latter played one Test for England in 1884 and turned out for Blackheath when he wasn't involved with the family side). In fact, Druitt was in such good odour with the cricketing establishment that he was elected a member of the MCC in 1884.

Druitt was placed on the Jack the Ripper short list because he was the preferred suspect of Sir Melville MacNaghten, Chief Constable of the Metropolitan Police. MacNaghten, who had not been directly involved in the police investigations, wrote a report in February 1894 which remained confidential until 1959. His main points linking Druitt to the murders were: the coincidences referred to above; Druitt's sexual proclivities (he was rumoured to be a homosexual); MacNaghten's unsubstantiated assertions that he had further evidence; and that Druitt's own family believed him to be the murderer.

So when Druitt's body weighed down by stones was found floating in the Thames on 31 December 1888, the facts fitted the interpretation that he had drowned himself through self-disgust and guilt. However, it actually appears that Druitt threw himself into the Thames because of something close to depression. He had just been fired from his school because of an unknown scandal, and his family had a history of mental illness. Amongst all the Ripper literature not many people favour MacNaghten's conclusions that were tenuous to say the least. Druitt was playing cricket through much of the Ripper period; he scored good runs, took good wickets and he was Treasurer and Secretary of Blackheath until his disappearance. Cricket followers would surely want to support one of their own. Umpire's verdict: Not out!

HOW TO ALWAYS WIN THE TOSS

W.G. was admired by his opponents for his outstanding cricket achievements but some had reservations about his conduct, which could be a bit sharp. On one occasion his side was in the field and, after the day's play, W.G. got chatting to one of the not-out batsmen. He told Grace that he was sure he had been out lbw to the last ball of the day but no one had appealed. The next morning, before the first ball was bowled, Grace shouted 'How's that!' and the batsman was given out to the last delivery of the previous evening.

Grace was a great believer in batting first. His dictum was 'When you win the toss – bat. If you are in doubt, think about it, then bat. If you have very big doubts, consult a colleague – then bat.' To ensure the odds of winning the toss were significantly in his favour, he patented

a little routine. He didn't call 'heads' or 'tails'; instead he called 'the Lady'. He used a coin with Queen Victoria on one side and Britannia on the other so, whichever way the coin came down, he would claim that he had won.

The bowler who bowled too well

Albert Trott and his benefit match

Albert Trott was a brilliantly talented cricketer with several unusual records both as a batsman and bowler. These included arguably playing too well in his own benefit match.

Born in Melbourne in 1873, he played Test cricket for Australia aged only 21. His Test debut, when he took eight for 43 and scored 38 and 72 (both not out), was stunning. He batted well in the next Test, too, although for some unexplained reason he didn't bowl. His third Test was less successful but he still had a batting average of 102.50 at the end of the series. Australia was due to tour England in 1896 but even though Trott's elder brother Harry was captain, Albert wasn't selected. In fact – and this has never been explained – after those three Tests he never played for Australia again, so his batting average of 102.50 is the highest achieved by any Australian, even the great Don.

In the same year, Trott decided to try his luck with an English county side and joined Middlesex. In both 1899 and 1900 he scored over 1,000 runs and took over 200 wickets; he was universally considered the best all-rounder of his time. In 1899 he did something truly remarkable – hitting a ball from Monty Noble over the Lord's pavilion, a feat never achieved before or since. Ironically, Noble was a prominent member of the Australian touring party for which Trott had not been selected. Trott, now available for England, was selected for England's 1898-99 tour of South Africa and performed creditably in two Tests, joining the elite group who have played in Tests for two countries.

Trott seems to have been gregarious and was not averse to a drink, even lifting a glass or two

with spectators on the boundary. From 1901 onwards his form began to decline due to fitness problems. Eventually in 1907, he became entitled to a benefit match against Somerset, the game in which he played too well – to his own detriment. In the fourth innings Somerset needed 264 to win; Trott made sure they never got anywhere near it. He finished the game off with one of the most remarkable individual performances in cricket history, first taking four wickets in consecutive balls (a double hat-trick) and then another hat-trick, the only person to have achieved that in the same innings. His seven for 20 was a wonderful achievement for Middlesex who won by 166 runs, but whether it was as wonderful for Trott is open to question. An early end to the game may have caused him to miss out on substantial benefit collections; Trott reportedly said that he 'bowled himself into the poorhouse.' It's a pity he couldn't have chosen some other game for this feat.

In cricketing terms it had been a grand finale but from then on it was downhill. He continued to play until 1910 and then became an umpire, but gave that up because of bad health. His wife left him, taking the children. In 1914, after a depressing spell in hospital, impoverished and scarcely able to walk, Albert shot himself. Aged only 41, he had become an early member of that unhappy club which found life hard to cope with outside the world of cricket.

BE CAREFUL HOW YOU SPELL MY NAME

***The New Zealander Bob Cunis (1941–2008) was a respectable Test cricketer who played 20 times for his country. He once scored 50, and once took six wickets, but never really hit the heights. Later he coached the national team. Perhaps his greatest claim to fame came when Alan Gibson commented on* Test Match Special*, 'This is Cunis at the Vauxhall end. Cunis, a funny sort of a name: neither one thing nor the other.' This bon mot has also been attributed to the peerless commentator John Arlott, but the original credit seems to belong to the editor and poet Alan Ross, in a report in* The Observer.**

Beethoven in at number eight

The mathematician who made up teams

G.H. Hardy was one of the most distinguished mathematicians of the first half of the twentieth century, holding important professorial posts at Oxford and Cambridge universities. Apart from his professional involvement with mathematics, he was totally obsessed with cricket. Indeed, the vocabulary of cricket spilled over into all aspects of his life: new acquaintances were instantly assessed for their qualities of 'spin', and intellectual achievement was measured in terms of the greatest batsman of the day, Jack Hobbs. To be in the 'Hobbs' class was a rare accolade and meant you were the best; in fact, it was quite a blow to his rating system when he had to introduce a Bradman class and re-rank everyone.

Hardy did not tend towards the romantic 'Play up, play up and play the game' view of cricket. As reported by the novelist and scientist C.P. Snow, Hardy once sharply observed: 'Cricket is the only game when you are playing against eleven of the other side and ten of your own.' Another sardonic Hardy remark also has the ring of truth about it: 'If you are nervous when you go in first, nothing restores your confidence so much as seeing the other man go out.'

Each day he studied the cricket

scores with intense concentration, so much so that the famous economist John Maynard Keynes said to him that if he had spent half an hour applying the same amount of care and attention to the stock exchange prices, he would have become a very rich man. Like many cricket lovers he enjoyed making up notional teams, although most of their members had never been anywhere near a cricket field. Here is a team sheet found after his death:

HOBBS
ARCHIMEDES
SHAKESPEARE
M ANGELO
NAPOLEON
H FORD
PLATO
BEETHOVEN
JOHNSON (JACK)
CHRIST (J)
CLEOPATRA

Jesus seems a little low in the batting order but then Hardy was a vehement atheist. Henry Ford was the founder of the Ford Motor Company, Jack Johnson the first African-American world heavyweight boxing champion (1908-15).

Another of his teams included the three members of the Trinity, identified as God (F), God (S) and God (HG), batting at nine, ten and eleven. There are plenty of other teams to be made up, such as this occupational Test team: Glenn Turner, Seymour Nurse, Keith Fletcher (capt), Mark Butcher, Farokh Engineer (wk), Keith Miller, Bob Barber, Ian Bishop, Terry Alderman, Peter Loader and Nick Cook. Twelfth Man: Michael Slater. Manager: Kerry Packer. As more than one Cook would break the rules, Nick's spin just shades it over

Alastair's opening skills with umpires David Shepherd and Mervyn Kitchen to give him the leg befores. And that's without including any Smiths who could make up an excellent team in themselves.

Hardy's mathematical power dropped away as he got older, but not his interest in cricket. On his deathbed he told his sister, who was reading to him from a history of Cambridge University cricket, 'If I knew that I was going to die today, I think I should still want to hear the cricket scores.' Many other cricket lovers would probably say the same.

LOSING IT ON AIR

Although cricket fans take the game seriously there is still time for banter, even if some of the humour can be at the schoolboy level. A commentator only has to mention 'rod' (Christopher Martin-Jenkins), 'leg over' and 'rubber' (Jonathan Agnew) and 'ball' (by anyone in almost any context) on air, and you can hear the sound of suppressed giggling in the background.

Sometimes the commentator can battle through without losing his composure; sometimes not. Jonathan Agnew and Brian Johnston couldn't utter a sensible word for minutes after Agnew's famous 'he didn't quite get his leg over' description of Botham stepping on his wicket. Apparently the nation came to a standstill too, as motorists stopped driving, convulsed with laughter.

Christopher Martin-Jenkins came to grief through a complicated metaphor involving a batsman fishing outside the off stump whilst trying to keep his rod down – cue much spluttering in the commentary

box. Agnew was waxing lyrical to Michael Vaughan about how to change the rubber covering on a bat handle when he came out with 'It's not easy putting a rubber on, is it?' Hilarity reigned.

Following the 'leg over' incident, the next most famous piece of commentary purportedly also involved Brian Johnston. During a Test, the West Indies fast bowler Michael Holding was about to bowl to the English batsman Peter Willey. Johnston is said to have set the scene by saying 'The bowler's Holding, the batsman's Willey.' However, **Wisden** ***says the story is apocryphal, there doesn't appear to be a BBC recording, and Johnston denied ever saying it.***

But he never denied saying 'Welcome to Leicester where the captain Ray Illingworth has just relieved himself at the pavilion end' or, after the New Zealand batsman Glenn Turner had been hit in a tender area, 'Turner looks a bit shaky and unsteady, but I think he's going to bat on... one ball left.'

The man who loved playing

The umpire with the bowling itch

In some respects, the 14-year career of the fast-medium bowler Dave Halfyard (1931-96) seems to be the epitome of the honest professional who plays very effectively at county level without ever quite looking like England material. But hidden within many so-called journeyman careers are often remarkable features and, in its way, Halfyard's was as noteworthy as any other.

Halfyard began playing for Kent in 1956 and was very successful for six years, taking 100 wickets in a season five times. But in 1962 he had a serious car crash on his way to a game and, after brave attempts at a comeback in league cricket, he retired from playing. Instead he became an umpire, joining the first-class umpires' list in 1967. However the bowling itch still remained and before a game he used to enjoy himself bowling in the nets at the county players – certainly not standard practice for umpires.

In an unlikely turn of events, on one of these occasions he was observed by Nottinghamshire who were impressed enough to consider offering him a contract. However it was a hard sell to the County committee who knew of his fitness difficulties: almost the whole committee had to watch him bowl for two hours before they were convinced. Halfyard promptly gave up his umpiring role and joined Nottinghamshire, the first and only umpire to have retired from cricket and then gone back to playing it.

He played another three years for Nottinghamshire, providing good service. In all first-class games, he took almost 1,000 wickets. His best figures were nine for 39, and he took ten wickets in a match 13 times. After retiring from first-class cricket in 1970, he continued to play Minor Counties cricket. As late as 1974, aged 43 and playing for Cornwall, he took 16 of the 19 Devon wickets to fall in the Minor Counties Championship match. He bowled 41 overs in the second innings with figures of eight for 58, only narrowly failing to force the victory.

At the same time as he was playing Minor Counties cricket for Cornwall, he resumed his umpiring career and stayed on the first-class list until 1994. He died in 1996 aged 65; he was still playing league cricket until a few weeks before his death. Journeyman or not, it is clear that here was a man who just loved to play cricket.

Once a 'keeper…

Appealing habits of old wicket-keepers

When retired players take up umpiring, it can be some time before they think like umpires rather than the players they once were. This is particularly true of former wicket-keepers, who have spent their entire careers appealing hopefully for catches.

The Essex player Bill Reeves told the story of Tommy Oates, who became an umpire in the 1920s after a long career spent keeping wicket for Nottinghamshire. In a match between MCC and Essex, Reeves was bowling at the end where Oates was umpiring. The batsman snicked it to the wicket-keeper and, caught up in the moment,

Oates reverted to his playing days behind the stumps and roared 'How's that!' Reeves signalled 'Out!' happily lifting his finger. It must have been a clear edge because the batsman accepted the decision and returned to the pavilion without argument.

Jack Board, a former England and Gloucestershire wicket-keeper, was umpiring at the Oval in the 1920s when a batsman edged the ball. Board appealed and raised his finger at the same time. On another occasion in a Test match, Leslie Ames, England's great wicket-keeper batsman of the 1930s, joined in the loud appeal for a catch behind. The trouble was that he wasn't the wicket-keeper or even the umpire but the batsman at the other end, and he was appealing against his own batting partner.

What W.G. doesn't tell you, Part 1

How Pooley missed the boat

W.G. Grace's *Cricketing Reminiscences*, written with Arthur Porritt and published in 1899, makes interesting reading, although in a discreet manner that wouldn't sell too many copies today. This and the immediately following story (*see* What W.G. doesn't tell you, Part 2) expand on two references in the *Reminiscences*. However they don't do anything like justice to the bizarre incidents they refer to, in one of which W.G. arguably behaved like a rogue.

Ted Pooley was the best English wicket-keeper of his day and was selected to tour Australia with James Lillywhite's side in 1876-77 for the first series of Australia-England Test matches. He was the only regular wicket-keeper and therefore certain to play, but got himself involved in an incident as sensational in its time as any cricketing scandal today.

The boat journey to Australia took in New Zealand where, amongst other games, the touring team was due to play Eighteen of Canterbury in Christchurch. According to the England bowler Alfred Shaw, in the bar the night before the match Pooley, who had form in this area, offered to bet £1 to a shilling that he could predict the individual score of every member of the home team; the bet was accepted by a certain Ralph Donkin.

Pooley simply named a duck as the score of each Canterbury batsman, which Shaw describes as 'a trick familiar to cricketers.' It was inevitable that the less talented local side would have a good number of ducks and for every duck Pooley would collect £1, while paying out only a shilling for each batsman who scored.

The odds were heavily stacked in his favour and he duly won the bet, expecting to collect about £10. However Donkin refused to pay on the grounds that it was a 'catch' bet. Pooley allegedly confronted and

assaulted him, and also reportedly trashed Donkin's clothes in his hotel room. He was arrested and had to face trial in Christchurch in April.

In the event Pooley and Bramall, the baggage man who was also accused, were found not guilty. But it was too late. The team had moved on and the first Test against Australia had already taken place, Australia winning by 45 runs and with England using a makeshift 'keeper.

Locals felt sorry for Pooley and collected £50 for him and Bramall, and presented Pooley with a gold ring. Pooley made his way back to England alone, having missed out on the honour of being England's first Test wicket-keeper. He found it hard to recover from the incident, played a few more years for Surrey but never again for England. He ended up in a workhouse where he died aged 65.

And what does W.G. have to say about Pooley's notoriety in his *Cricketing Reminiscences*? Surely it was worth something more than 'Pooley's retirement robbed the Surrey team of an invaluable wicket-keeper'?

What W.G. doesn't tell you, Part 2

The episode of the kidnapped player

In the second 'What W. G. doesn't tell you' episode (*see* What W.G. doesn't tell you, Part 1), W.G. has a little more to say in his *Reminiscences* about the main character, Billy Midwinter. However he has nothing to say, strangely, about the so-called 'kidnapping' incident in which W.G. himself took a leading part.

Midwinter was born in Gloucestershire in 1851 and emigrated with his family to Australia when he was nine. He was an all-rounder and good enough to play for Australia in the Inaugural Test against England in 1877 (the one Pooley missed because of the betting scam). Midwinter played well in the drawn series and later in the year came to England and played for W.G.'s county, Gloucestershire, for which he was qualified by birth.

The following year Midwinter was selected for the Australia side to tour England and played in some of their early games. W.G., however, thought that he had prior claim to the player as Midwinter had 'promised to play for Gloucestershire in all our matches.' Things came to a head when he included Midwinter in the Gloucestershire side to play Surrey.

This is how Grace tells it: 'On June 20, when the Gloucestershire men arrived at the Oval to play Surrey, I received a message to the effect that Midwinter would be absent, as he was playing for the Australians at Lord's. In consequence of his defection, Gloucestershire mustered only ten men. I immediately started off for Lord's, where I found Midwinter with his pads on, waiting to bat. After some persuasion he returned with me to the Oval to play for Gloucestershire.'

The alternative version of events has W.G. leaping into a taxi –

accompanied by 'persuasion' in the burly forms of his brother E.M. and Arthur Bush, the Gloucestershire wicket-keeper and an England rugby international forward – and dashing off to Lord's. The padded-up Midwinter was seized and the cab raced back to the Oval. The Australians immediately set after

them and confronted W.G. at the Oval, although the Aussies were unable to recover their man. A lengthy war of words then took place between Australia's management and Gloucestershire. Eventually tempers cooled, W.G. apologised, and there was a rapprochement.

However W.G. had won the war, as Midwinter now threw in his lot with Gloucestershire and England. In 1881-82 he toured Australia and played four Tests, becoming the first of the small number of cricketers to play at Test level for two countries, and the only one to have played for Australia against England and vice versa.

You might think that was enough to be going on with but (hard to believe) after a couple of years in England, he returned to Australia and from 1883 to 1887 played more Tests for them – against England, of course. Ultimately Midwinter had a sad fate: his wife and two of his children died and he had little success in business. He became 'hopelessly insane' and died in an asylum in Melbourne in 1890, aged only 39.

Writing in 1899, W.G. and his ghostwriter Porritt knew all this, of course, but they recorded Midwinter's subsequent history in the short phrase: 'Midwinter's return to Australia weakened the bowling.' This barely scratched the surface.

RUN OUT BY JULIUS CAESAR

To cricket aficionados, the name Julius Caesar does not refer to the Roman general of the first century BC, but to a highly regarded cricketer of the mid-nineteenth century and member of the All-England XI. On one occasion Caesar was playing for the United XI against a country XXII on a small ground where a coconut shy had been set up in the outfield for the amusement of the spectators. With the XXII down to their last pair, the game was almost all over. However the batsmen were stubborn, the evening was drawing in, and when it began to rain, it looked like they would achieve a draw. But Caesar was able to win it for his team with a piece of quick thinking. When one of the batsmen hit the ball past him, he chased after it towards the boundary. Stumbling into some coconuts on the way, he picked one up and flung it back to the wicket-keeper, Tom Lockyer, with the batsman out of his ground. In the rain and the gloom, no one noticed the substitution as Lockyer whipped off the bails, tucked the coconut inside his shirt and ran for the tent.

Golden oldies

Old enough and good enough

Once there was just three-day cricket, then one-day games were added to the schedule and now Twenty20 matches. The intensity and volume of modern-day cricket fixtures means that career spans have gradually shortened.

A few decades ago players were often playing into their 40s, and some even into their 50s and beyond. W.G. played from 1865 to 1908 when he was 60. Wilfred Rhodes (Yorkshire and England) played from 1898 to 1930, retiring at 52. He scored very nearly 40,000 runs, played in 1,110 games (easily a record) and batted for England in every position from one to 11. Sir Jack Hobbs (Surrey and England) played 834 games from 1905 to 1934 and retired in his 50s, much the same as his lifetime batting average. At the end of the First World War, when he was 37 and many cricketers would have been thinking of retiring, Hobbs played on and scored more than 100 centuries, finishing with a career total of 199.

The Middlesex player Fred Titmus, who began his first-class career in 1949, is one of the few players of modern times to have played in five different decades. He was semi-retired in August 1982 when he dropped into the Middlesex changing room at Lord's, was spotted by the Middlesex captain Mike Brearley and was persuaded to play. He had played county cricket only occasionally since 1976, but still performed creditably. Another career spanning five decades was that of the Yorkshire, Somerset and England cricketer Brian Close, who played from 1949 to 1986. However, the undoubted winner in this category is C.K. Nayudu, India's first Test captain, an aggressive batsman who made his debut in 1916 and played his last game in 1964 aged 69, thus playing first-class cricket across six decades. Of players active at the start of the 2012 English cricket season Mark Ramprakash of Surrey, beginning his 26th season, was 42, and Robert Croft of Glamorgan, starting his 24th season, was 41 – but they are very much the exceptions.

Two extraordinary career records deserve a mention here. The Rev. Reginald Moss had played a few

games for Oxford University in the 1880s and one first-class game for Liverpool and District in 1893. Then he inexplicably played one game for Worcestershire in 1925 at the age of 57, predictably performing rather poorly. This gap of 32 years between appearances is easily the greatest ever that has been recorded in first-class cricket.

Raja Maharaja Singh, the first Indian Governor of Bombay, made his debut in November 1950 at Bombay captaining the Bombay Governor's XI against a very strong Commonwealth team that included Jim Laker, Sonny Ramadhin, George Tribe and Derek Shackleton. The game had first-class status and the moment he set foot on the field to bat in the first innings at an eyebrow-raising 75 years old, he set two records unlikely to be challenged. He became the oldest person to make his first-class debut and also the oldest person to have played first-class cricket, leaving W.G.'s 60 and Nayudu's 69 in his wake. He was out to Laker after scoring 4 runs, probably gifted to him as the usual polite gesture from a touring team to a local dignitary. Having achieved this much, he did not take any further part in the match.

Outside the first-class arena, the pressure is less and cricket can be played and enjoyed to a very great age. Possibly the outstanding example is Jack Hyams of Nomads CC. Born in 1919, he played until 2010, scoring more runs – almost 130,000 – in more games than anyone else in cricket. He scored a century in seven successive decades, starting in 1934 aged 14. Another golden oldie was the late Reg Harris who was still keeping wicket for Bugbrooke CC, Northamptonshire, in 2003 when he was almost 93.

Twenty20 fiasco
An offer that should have been refused

The average cricket lover must have blinked in disbelief at the spectacle. A helicopter had landed on the sacred turf of Lord's, disgorging a smartly dressed business type, then a very large and heavy-looking Perspex box. Shortly afterwards, the box reappeared indoors surrounded by some of the great and the good of England and West Indies cricket. Now it could be seen that it was packed with a large number of neatly stacked dollar bills – to the value of $20 million. The producers of *The Godfather* might have envied the scene.

It was June 2008 and Sir Allen Stanford, a Texas businessman with substantial business interests in the Caribbean, had come to town to help solve one of English cricket's biggest problems. The IPL (Indian Premier League) was getting under way and its riches were likely to prove irresistible to English players. This would bring them into conflict with the ECB who wanted these players available for their own games.

A counter-attraction Twenty20 competition under the ECB's own control was needed. As well as England the West Indies, whose board was going through another period of disarray, were likely participants in the new contest. Stanford had strong contacts there; he had even re-built a cricket ground in Antigua known locally as 'Sticky Wicket Stadium'. Stanford agreed to finance a five-year deal for this competition with a prize fund worth more than £70 million. With that kind of prize money, the thinking was that it shouldn't be hard to attract another couple of countries to make it a four-way series.

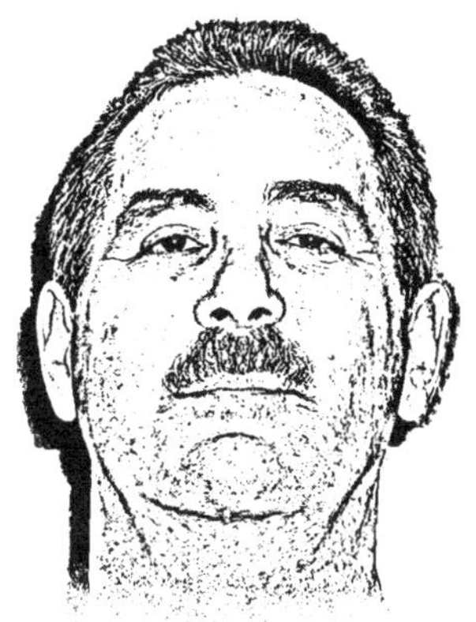

The first series took place in October and November 2008. Despite the riches on offer, none of the other major cricket-playing countries such as India, South Africa or Australia wanted to take part. Trinidad and Tobago, and Middlesex – winners of the 2008 Twenty20 Cup in England – were brought in to make up numbers.

In the grand finale England were to play the West Indies, called the Stanford Super Stars for the occasion. Stanford looked very content in the VIP stand, chatting up the wives and girlfriends of the English team. Some very good players were on show but the occasion fell flat as England, who seemed to come blinking into the sunlight as if unsure what they were doing there, scored only 99 which the Super Stars knocked off inside 13 overs. It was winner-takes-all, so each of the winning team won $1 million, with a further $1 million split among the reserves. Never had selection for a team been worth so much – and rarely had so much been earned for doing so little.

Early in the next year doubts about Stanford's probity began to surface. The ECB distanced itself from the businessman as quickly as possible and the remaining four series never took place. Subsequently Stanford – now stripped of his knighthood – has been found guilty of a $7 billion investment fraud. Observers used words like 'tacky' and 'vulgar' to describe the episode. For an organisation that prided itself on the highest standards in all its dealings on and off the field, it is generally agreed that English cricket's involvement with Allen Stanford was not its finest hour.

LUMPY OR BUMPY?

One of cricket's earliest characters was Edward Stevens (1735–89), universally known as 'Lumpy', even on scorecards. According to the cricket historian F.S. Ashley-Cooper, Lumpy earned his nickname either 'because he was so fat', or 'because he did once eat a whole apple-pie', which adds up to much the same thing. Lumpy was the most highly regarded bowler of his era and famed for his accuracy. In the days of wickets with only two stumps, it was Lumpy who bowled the famous Hambledon batsman John Small three times through the middle

of the wicket without dislodging the bail, resulting in the introduction of a third stump (see *The iron frame*).

These days the home side chooses the pitch site and prepares it, but in Lumpy's time it was the visitors' choice. John Nyren, the cricketer and writer, pointed out the advantages in The Progress of Cricket. *'Be careful to suit your bowling,' he wrote. He advised taking the wind and slope into account and putting on your fastest bowler 'when a cloud is passing over' as this 'frequently affects the sight of a striker.' Lumpy was such a master of picking a good site for his bowling that it was remembered in a verse: 'For honest Lumpy did allow, he ne'er would pitch but o'er a brow.' Perhaps, as some say, this is where the nickname 'Lumpy' originated, but if so, 'Bumpy' might have been a more obvious choice?*

In any case, his talent earned him a job as a gardener on the estate of the Earl of Tankerville. His Lordship, a cricketer himself, had such confidence in Lumpy that he took a wager on his bowling ability. He bet the substantial sum of £100 that Lumpy could pitch a ball on a feather, one ball in four. He won his bet.

Help yourself

Wellington serve up 77-run over

The most number of runs that can be scored off a normal over is 36. But 36 is only a notional maximum; by bowling deliberate no-balls and wides an over can theoretically last for ever, and 36 has been exceeded at different levels of cricket. This is a tactic used from time to time to provide a batting side with extra runs to get them interested in chasing a total and winning a game which otherwise might end in a draw.

An over which took this tactic to extremes occurred in the Wellington v. Canterbury game in a Shell Trophy match played at Christchurch, New Zealand, in February 1990. Wellington, in with a chance of winning the championship, decided to offer Canterbury the opportunity to win a game otherwise heading for a draw. The Wellington captain asked his bowler, Bert Vance, to bowl high, wide and handsome no-balls for the Canterbury batsmen to hit for six. This they did with relish. There were 22 balls in the over, 17 no-balls and five fair deliveries – only five because in the welter of no balls and sixes the umpire lost track and finished a delivery short. Eight sixes and six fours were hit and a total of 77 was scored. One of the batsmen, Lee Germon, scored 160 not out, his highest score in a first-class game – if it could be called that. Despite the shenanigans, the game ended in a draw but Canterbury still won the title.

The first person to score 36 off a six-ball over in first-class cricket was the West Indian Gary Sobers, perhaps the finest all-round cricketer the game has ever known. The unfortunate bowler was Glamorgan's Malcolm Nash at St Helen's Cricket Ground, Swansea, on 31 August 1968. The Indian Test cricketer Ravi Shastri is the only other player to achieve this in a first-class match, in 1985.

Testing the boundaries

How Somerset were too clever for their own good

In cricket, the difference between what is acceptable and what is sharp practice, even if within the rules, can be paper-thin and cricketers have always tested the dividing line. Earlier in the book, the story is told of a ball being rolled underarm along the ground to prevent the possibility of a six being hit and the game tied (*see* When underarm was underhand). However, that act of dubious sportsmanship at least came at the end of a full game of cricket – and it was legal, although the laws were changed soon after. But what are we to make of this?

In May 1979, in the group stages of the Benson & Hedges Cup, Worcester were playing Somerset at home. The situation was that Somerset could lose the game and still qualify for the next round as long as they weren't overtaken on strike rate. The Somerset captain Brian Rose naturally wanted to protect that position, so he did some thinking and came up with a plan, knowing that it would be highly controversial. Indeed, he went so far as to check its legality with the secretary of the TCCB. Effectively, he was told that his plan was within the laws of the game, but not within its spirit.

Somerset won the toss – ideal for Rose's strategy – and chose to bat. Rose and Peter Denning opened the batting. After one over the score was 1 for no wicket, the run resulting from a no-ball. At this point Rose put his plan into action: he declared the Somerset innings closed. After the ten-minute interval it took Worcestershire ten balls to score the 2 runs needed for victory. The game had lasted 18 minutes.

Somerset had lost the game but the run rate had been protected and they would qualify for the next round. Spectators arriving at the ground and looking forward to seeing innings from great players like Viv Richards and Ian Botham of Somerset, and Glenn Turner and Younis Ahmed of Worcestershire, were told that the game had already finished. Mike Vokins, Worcestershire's secretary, was disgusted and refunded the gate money. Members of the public, some of whom had driven some distance, were furious. A schoolteacher criticised the example it set to the group of schoolchildren he had brought to the match.

Rose said that what he had done was perfectly legal and blamed the rules for making such a course of action possible. Somerset's committee and players supported Rose, in public anyway, but virtually no one else did. The TCCB had no doubt: what Somerset had done was definitely 'not cricket', even if within the rules. The team was expelled from the competition and the rules were changed to prevent sides from declaring in one-day games. So Somerset ended up with the worst of all possible outcomes. The irony was that if they had played the game 'properly', even if they had lost, the other results meant they would have qualified comfortably anyway.

Unexpected fame at 37

The player who rose and fell without trace

It was once said of the leading media personality, Sir David Frost, that 'he rose without trace.' Whether or not that's true, the description certainly fits Douglas Ward Carr (1872-1950). In one magical season in 1909 he went from unknown club cricketer to playing for England and performing creditably against the Australians in an Ashes Test. The editor of a boy's comic desperate for a plot would surely have rejected the storyline as totally implausible.

Carr had played cricket first for Brasenose College, Oxford University, without making the university team, and then club cricket for a number of years in the Maidstone area of Kent where he was a schoolmaster. In 1906, aged 34, he began practising the new mystery delivery, the 'googly'. Its inventor, Bernard Bosanquet, had been successful with it but hadn't played for England since 1905. It took a couple of years for Carr to perfect, but by August 1908 he had 'really got the thing going'.

In May the following year his impact in club cricket was so great that he was offered a trial by Kent. He made his first-class debut against his old university, aged 37, and took seven wickets in the match. By July he was playing for the Gentlemen against the Players, taking eight wickets in the match. It began to look like he was Bosanquet's successor, and with Australia 2-1 up in the Ashes series, the newspapers and the public applied pressure upon the selectors to put him in the Test team.

He was picked for the England squad for the Old Trafford Test but didn't make the final side. He was then selected to play at the Oval in August, one of the oldest players to make a Test debut. His first-class experience amounted to three matches. Opening the bowling with S.F. Barnes in both innings, he took seven wickets in the drawn match, the most by an England bowler in the game. However he was quite expensive, giving away well over 100 runs in each innings. In the county championship, he finished the season with 95 wickets and Kent won the title.

For whatever reason, his period as flavour of the month ended and he was never selected by England again. He continued to play for Kent until 1914 when his career was brought to an end by the outbreak of the First World War. He died in 1950 aged 78. After those few brilliant, unexpected years when he had played for England, been selected as one of *Wisden's* Cricketers of the Year and helped his county to win three championship titles, unlike Sir David Frost, he sank without trace.

Well batted, you're dropped!

When the best wasn't good enough

The news is out: you've been selected for your first Test match. You're very nervous and keen to do well. If you're a batsman, you want to score a century and join an exclusive club. If you're a bowler, you just want to get your name indelibly in the wickets column, share in the high-fives, and see if you can get some more.

The day comes; miraculously it

all goes brilliantly. You score 112 like Andy Ganteaume for the West Indies in 1948; or 107 and 56 like Rodney Redmond for New Zealand in 1973. You take five for 37 in the first innings and six for 59 in the second like the leg break and googly bowler Charles Marriott for England in 1933; or seven for 95 like William 'Gobo' Ashley of South Africa in 1889. Everyone says you have a glittering Test career ahead of you. Except that the selectors never ring again. You've played the only Test you're ever going to.

Why were none of these players ever chosen again? In Marriott's case he was already 37 when he made his debut and popularly known as 'Father' Marriott. His batting and his fielding weren't really up to scratch, although no one has ever taken more wickets in their first Test. Ganteaume was an injury replacement and was criticised for slow batting in a drawn game against England that the West Indies may well have thought they should have won. In any case, the West Indies with Weekes, Worrell and Walcott at three, four and five weren't short of batting talent. At least Ganteaume had the consolation of finishing with the highest-ever Test batting average of 112, beating Bradman's 99.94 quite comfortably. Of course, Bradman had also scored the little matter of 6,884 runs. Marriott, too, finished with the best-ever Test career bowling average of 8.72.

Rodney Redmond was unfortunate in that his scores were made in the final match of a three-match series against Pakistan in New Zealand in 1973. Next was a tour of England and, as you'd expect, he was selected for it. However, he wore contact lenses and those caused him so much trouble that he lost form and never made the Test side, and in fact didn't play first-class cricket much longer.

The whole first-class career of 'Gobo' Ashley, a medium-paced left-armer, consisted of five games including his one Test. He never had a chance to add to his seven wickets in the first innings as England batted only once, winning by an innings and 202 runs. Maybe he suffered in comparison to another left-armer, Johnny Briggs, who took 15 wickets in the match for England, all but one of them bowled.

Outside the Test arena, it is worth remembering the 207 scored by the 18-year-old Australian Norman Callaway for New South Wales in 1915, his only first-class innings. Regarded as an outstanding prospect, he never had the chance to pursue a cricketing career as he was killed in action in France in 1917. His one innings has left him with the highest first-class batting average ever.

THE TEST OPENER WHO WAS NEVER OUT

Andy Lloyd, the former Warwickshire and England batsman, holds one of those Test records which are meat and drink to lovers of cricket curiosities but would rather be forgotten by the record holder.

In the 1984 Test series against England, the West Indies were probably at their peak with batsmen like Viv Richards, Gordon Greenidge and Desmond Haynes, and a pace attack including Malcolm Marshall, Michael Holding and Joel Garner, three of the greatest fast bowlers of all time. Lloyd had batted well in the immediately preceding ODI series, top-scoring in two of England's three innings although without reaching a half-century. On this basis the slightly desperate England selectors gave him the unenviable task of opening the batting for England on his home ground, Edgbaston.

Lloyd very quickly discovered the gulf between the intensity of one-day and Test cricket. He had been in for 33 minutes and made 10 runs when a bouncer from Marshall hit him on the head. Despite his helmet, he was taken to hospital suffering from double vision and missed the rest of the match. He did not play cricket again until the following season and was never selected again for England. Although very unfortunate for Lloyd, it does enable him to claim that he is the only Test opening batsman never to have been dismissed.

For the remainder of the series, England tried out other openers including Chris Broad and Paul Terry. The latter's Test career was almost a carbon copy of Lloyd's. Given another chance after an unproductive debut, in the second Test a ball from Winston Davis broke his arm. At the end of the innings with Lamb on 98 not out, Terry bravely

returned to the wicket with his arm in a sling to enable Lamb to reach his century. Sensibly Terry did not bat in the second innings. England was too far behind to make it worthwhile, losing by an innings and going on to lose the series 5-0. He never played for England again.

Pass the hat, please

Three in a row does the trick

The definition of hat-trick is fairly straightforward: taking three wickets in three consecutive balls. The term dates back to 1858 when a collection was held for H.H. Stephenson after he took three wickets in three balls. Some say that a hat was passed around the spectators and the collection handed over to the bowler, but the balance of opinion is that a hat was bought with the proceeds and given to Stephenson. There have been only 39 hat-tricks in over 2,000 Test matches, and at any level of cricket they are a treasured rarity for almost everyone except the batsmen involved. However cricket, being cricket, always manages to throw up some strange variations on the theme.

Against the West Indies in 1988, the famously aggressive Australian fast bowler Merv Hughes, with the monster moustaches, performed an unusual hat-trick across three overs and two innings. He took a wicket with the last ball of an over and then another wicket with the first ball of his next over – that happened to be the last wicket of the innings. When the West Indies began their second innings, he opened the bowling and took the wicket of Gordon Greenidge with his first ball to give him this unique hat-trick. He deserved it because he took 13 wickets in the match – although Australia still lost.

The Yorkshire slow bowler Horace Fisher was the first to achieve a hat-trick of lbws in 1932 against Somerset. The umpire involved was Alec Skelding, famous for his humorous asides. On one occasion, asked to decide on a run out, Skelding said 'That was a photo-finish and as there isn't time to develop the plate I shall say not out.' When Fisher appealed for the third lbw, Skelding took time to think about it, aware that he was about to make history. Finally he said, 'As God's my witness, that's out, too,' before raising his finger. 'I was never more sure that I was right in each case,' he said afterwards. Lbws are amongst the rarest forms of hat-tricks, although the great South Africa and Gloucestershire all-rounder Mike Procter achieved such a hat-trick twice.

Despite this sounding a contradiction in terms, there have been hat-tricks not involving a bowler. An outstanding, probably unique, hat-trick was achieved in 2005 by Josh Bateson, fielding for Horsforth Cricket Club's (near Leeds) under-11 side; their opponents were the Old Leodensians (Old Leos for short). In three consecutive balls, Josh ran out three Old Leos batsmen with direct hits – two at one end and the third at the other. No one has been able to find another example of such amazing accuracy.

For hat-trick complexity, the 2011 World Cup game between Ireland and the Netherlands is probably

unmatched. In this instance four wickets fell in three balls. The Netherlands batted first and were in the middle of the last over of their innings. Thanks to a fast hundred by Ryan ten Doeschate they had reached the competitive total of 305 but were naturally pressing to get every run they could.

On ball four of the over and with the score at 304 for six, Atse Buurman, batting at seven, tried to steal a run to the wicket-keeper off a wide but was run out, although the wide counted as a run. The wide also meant it was still ball four and off the re-bowled delivery the new batsman, Seelar at number nine, was run out attempting a risky single. On ball five Raja, the number ten at the non-striker's end, called Bukhari the striker for a run but Bukhari, a bit of a hitter, wanted to retain the strike and didn't budge. So Raja was run out without facing a ball. Off ball six, the last ball of the innings, Bukhari swung it away to mid-wicket and was run out going for an impossible second. And that is how, in cricket, there can be four run outs in three balls.

IT'S JUST NOT KILIKITI!

In Samoa, cricket (or 'kilikiti') was taken up with great passion in the late nineteenth century, albeit with the basics substantially modified. Teams could consist of 200 or 300 men a side and games could last for weeks – although sometimes they were merely a cover for a raid on a neighbouring island. Bats would not have passed the Hambledon test (**see** ***The iron frame) and there were three batsmen at each end (one to bat and the other two to act as running relays). In addition, poor fielding was punished on the spot by an official equipped with a long whip to scourge the offender. Nevertheless, kilikiti proved so popular with the Samoans that all other activities, including work in the fields, were completely neglected and the King was forced to issue the following proclamation:***

THE LAW REGARDING CRICKET

To All The Districts of Samoa, Notice

1. It is strictly prohibited for a village to travel and play cricket with another village.
2. It is strictly prohibited for two villages to play cricket together.
3. It is also prohibited for a village to play cricket among themselves.
4. Should any village or district fail to keep this law in any respect, they will be fined a sum not exceeding forty-five dollars, or in default be sent to jail for three months with hard labour.

MALIETOA, THE KING OF SAMOA
RESIDENCE OF THE KING, APIA
JUNE 20, 1890

A similar edict was later issued in Tonga.

No room for sentiment

Easier to survive a war than the umpire's decision

There is a little-known form of dismissal in cricket called timed out. It exists in order to prevent delaying tactics by the batting side and basically states that after a wicket has fallen, the incoming batsman has three minutes (it used to be two) to reach the crease. Dismissal of this kind is so rare that there are only four instances in first-class cricket, each one a story in itself.

Playing against Durham UCCE in 2003, Nottinghamshire were batting strongly. Andrew Harris, their number 11, had suffered a groin strain and hadn't changed, thinking he would not be required. However the middle order collapsed and Harris was told to bat. He flung on his clothes but was too late reaching the middle – he was timed out. His teammate, Chris Read, wasn't very pleased – he was left stranded on 94 not out.

In the Howa Bowl game between Eastern Province and Transvaal in February 1988, Andrew Jordaan, opening for Eastern Province, was

0 not out at close of play. After torrential rain overnight, road conditions were so difficult the next morning that Jordaan couldn't reach the ground for start of play. He was subsequently timed out.

In September 2002 Vasbert Drakes, a West Indian fast bowler, was trying to travel from Colombo, Sri Lanka, where he had been playing in the ICC Champions Trophy, to East London, South Africa, to play for Border. This was a short hop of 4,400 miles (7,000kms). His plane

was delayed and, even though he was dropped lower and lower in the batting order, he never made it, finding himself in the unique position of being timed out whilst in mid-air.

In December 1997 at the Barabati Stadium in Cuttack, India, Tripura were batting against Orissa. When they lost their ninth wicket, the umpires called for a drinks break with the Tripura number 11, Hemulal Yadav, last man in. However, Yadav was still deep in conversation with his team manager on the edge of the boundary when play was due to restart and was given out.

If these cases contain a light-hearted element, another similar incident has rather more serious overtones. Harold Heygate had played a few games for Sussex between 1903 and 1905 but hadn't been successful and had dropped out of first-class cricket. During the First World War, he sustained leg wounds and suffered badly from either arthritis or rheumatism.

In 1919, when first-class cricket resumed, he went to Taunton to watch his old team play Somerset. Sussex turned up short of a player and asked Heygate to play. However when Somerset batted first, it rapidly became clear that he was effectively immobile and was excused fielding. When Sussex batted, he went in at 11 and was out for a duck.

Understandably, at this point Heygate seems to have felt that, having made a brave effort, it was now proving a bit much; he therefore didn't change into whites for the second day. In their second innings, Sussex needed only a very manageable 105 to win, and at 103 for six the game was in their grasp. But they lost two wickets at that score and another on 104.

The totals were now level. If the crippled Heygate could make it out to the middle, Sussex might yet score the winning run. He actually made the attempt, buckling on pads over his suit. But his preparation and painful efforts to reach the middle were taking a long time. Someone on the Somerset side appealed and the umpire gave him timed out.

The game ended a tie and Sussex were mightily displeased. According to a note in their scorebook: 'With regard to umpire Street's decision that Heygate should not bat, the time was 4 o'clock, so still 3 hours to play. Heygate was ready to play and was at the wicket when Street decided that as he had exceeded the two minutes he could not bat. He was ready to play and he did not call "Play".'

Public opinion and sympathy fell firmly on Heygate's side as a wounded survivor of the Great War. The MCC looked into the decision but ruled that the umpire was right. Eventually it was decided to change the scorebook entry to show Heygate was 'out, absent', although modern records show him as 'absent hurt.' That is why this incident is not thought of today as an example of timed out.

AN UNUSUAL EXCUSE

In his book* Chappelli has the Last Laugh, *former Australian Test captain Ian Chappell tells how during their game against North Zone on the 1969–70 tour of India, the hometown umpiring was beginning to seriously irritate the Australian tourists. In particular, the spin bowler John Gleeson was receiving no favourable decisions.

Finally the opening batsman, Vinay Lamba, snicked one; Gleeson and the wicket-keeper, Brian Taber, roared an appeal. The Indian umpire made no move to give Lamba out; he was only two short of his 50, after all.

The Australians all stared at him and one or two began to advance from the outfield to reinforce the appeal. Under pressure, the umpire's finger was finally raised. The players grouped around to congratulate Gleeson and Taber but were surprised to be joined by the umpire. 'Oh Mr Gleeson,' he said, 'I am sorry to have taken so long over that decision but there was a strong wind blowing against me and it took a long time for the snick to carry to my end.'

A doubtful action

Was cricket's most successful bowler a chucker?

Before the introduction of the DRS (Decision Review System) in 2009 lightened the pressure on umpires, there was a period when it seemed as if one or two of them were looking for confrontation. Take the case of the Australian umpire Ross Emerson who umpired ten ODIs from 1996 to 1999.

His very first match was between Sri Lanka and the West Indies in Brisbane in January 1996. Sri Lanka's team included the off spinner Muttiah Muralitharan (Murali) who, along with the Australian Shane Warne, was the most effective spin bowler of his time. Murali's bowling action had always been controversial: in the previous month he had been no-balled seven times for throwing in a Test match by another Australian umpire, Darrell Hair. Sir Donald Bradman called it bad umpiring and said 'clearly Murali does not throw the ball.'

Standing in his first ODI less than two weeks later, Emerson also called Murali for throwing – also seven times. It may possibly have been a pre-determined decision on Emerson's part. He went on 'calling' Murali even when the player switched to bowling leg breaks, which experts say cannot be bowled with a bent arm. As a result, Sri Lanka were unable to play Murali in any more games on that tour.

The following month Murali underwent controlled tests at a laboratory. His controversial action was attributed to a congenital deformity of the elbow that created the illusion that he was throwing. Murali was now free to bowl again without being called for chucking, as umpires knew his action had been officially cleared. All except Emerson, it seems.

In an ODI between Sri Lanka and England in January 1999, the umpire again called Murali for throwing. The Sri Lanka captain almost led his team off the field but was persuaded not to; eventually Sri Lanka won the game with two balls to spare. However it was not a good game for Emerson, who made several wrong decisions that arguably cost England the match. He gave a seven-ball over, and awarded a six for a Sri Lanka shot that clearly bounced inside the boundary. Worst of all, he refused to consult the third umpire for a camera review on a run out decision. The television replays revealed he had called wrong and should have referred. The reprieved batsman, Mahela Jayawardene, was on 33 at the time and went to make 120 and to win the match for Sri Lanka.

Over the years, Murali had to undergo four sets of tests, including ones in a rigid arm brace. When he passed these, many of his critics withdrew their objections. The consequences for cricket were interesting as the tests showed that, if Murali was throwing, so had virtually every bowler in the history of the game. According to the lab, it was actually physically impossible to bowl according to the International Cricket Council's (ICC's) standard of five degrees. New tolerances were set at 15 per cent and all variations of Murali's deliveries, including his new mystery ball, the doosra, fell within this revised standard.

While Murali never quite succeeded in persuading everyone, he convinced those who mattered and played until 2011 when he retired having taken the highest number of wickets in Tests (800) and ODIs (534). He certainly outlasted Ross Emerson. After the England game it was discovered that the umpire was off work for a stress-related illness. He was stood down from the panel of umpires and never officiated at international level again.

The most exalted hat-trick

Bertie's King-sized victims

The most exalted hat-trick, going on social rather than cricketing status, was a royal one and involved one King bowling out three other Kings. According to *Wisden* in its obituary of George VI, it took place 'on the private ground on the slopes below Windsor Castle'. The bowler was the future George VI, known as 'Bertie', and the three rabbits were the reigning monarch, Edward VII, and the future George V and Edward VIII. *Wisden* does not provide us with a date, but since Edward VII died in 1910 and George VI was born in 1895, it might have been around 1905. None of the monarchs had much of a track record in cricket: before he was king, George V had played for his ship HMS *Bacchante* in a game in Fiji but was demoted to the

Second XI for the next game, which rather speaks for itself. The ball used to play the royal hat-trick eventually found its way to the mess room of the Royal Naval College, Dartmouth.

One rather keen cricketing member of the Royal Family of that era was Prince Christian Victor of Schleswig-Holstein, a grandson of Queen Victoria. Thanks to his single appearance for I Zingari against the Gentlemen of England in 1887, he is the only member of the Royal Family to have played first-class cricket. He just missed a Blue at Oxford but was successful while overseas, playing for the Army. He died on service in Pretoria in 1900, aged 33.

The most important member of the Royal Family to have seriously interested himself in the game is almost certainly Frederick, Prince of Wales (1707-51). It comes as a surprise that he took to cricket at all since he was born in Hanover and didn't arrive in Great Britain until he was 21. He began to attend games in the 1730s, although possibly as much for the gambling opportunities as for the cricket itself. Protocol deemed that games could not start until he was present. In one game in July 1735, the cricket historian H.T. Waghorn (1842-1930) says that 'the Earl (of Middlesex) came into the field about eleven o'clock... but the Prince did not come till one.' Stakes were vast: in this game and one earlier that same month, the prize money was £1,000 per game. The Earl's Kentish Men beat HRH's London Club on both occasions, probably compensating for the two-hour wait. The Prince himself occasionally played and it is said that he died after being hit on the head by a ball. If this is true, he is surely the most exalted victim from playing cricket.

SIGHTSCREEN WITH A DIFFERENCE

It is one of cricket's more frustrating episodes. The batsman takes his stance for the next ball but suddenly steps back as the bowler, having run in from 30yds (25m), is in mid-delivery stride. He then waves his bat irritably in the general direction of the pavilion to indicate that something has broken the trance-like state of concentration in which he must be cocooned to play a delivery.

Everyone swivels to see the cause of his aggravation. Quite often it is a well-padded spectator who is precariously carrying a large tray of drinks back to his seat and has walked behind the bowler's arm, despite all the signs requesting him not to do so during an over. Or sometimes it is a window reflecting the sunlight directly into the batsman's eyes. It seems to take an age to deal with the disruption.

In 2005, in a Test between New Zealand and Sri Lanka in Napier, New Zealand, the problem was created by an unusual source – the umpires themselves. The Sri Lankan fast bowler Lasith Malinga has an unusual roundarm action: he bowls from a point about the same height as his shoulder but an arm's length away from his body. The New Zealanders had not played him before in Test cricket and couldn't sight him. They eventually concluded that his arm was getting lost against the umpires' black uniforms. The issue had already arisen on the first day of the game, when the umpires had been asked to remove their dark ties because they were a similar colour to the ball; this they had agreed to do.

Then on the last day of the match, when New Zealand were struggling with Malinga's unfamiliar style, the New Zealand captain Stephen Fleming had a further request. Would Steve Bucknor, the umpire at Malinga's end, mind changing his black trousers for lighter-coloured ones? To make the point, one of the New Zealand batsmen beckoned to his dressing room for a pair of light-coloured trousers to be brought out for the umpire. Whether for reasons

of modesty or otherwise, this time Bucknor did mind. So instead, a large white sweater was produced. Would Bucknor agree to wrap this about his waist? No problem, said Bucknor, and this unusual but workable sightscreen solved the Malinga problem and the match was able to proceed.

Son of a Gunn

Well done, relatively speaking

Families sometimes have enough cricket talent to make up a family team (*see* All in the family). This has never happened at first-class level but close relatives have nevertheless thrown up notable class curiosities. For example, one 1933 Middlesex-Somerset match included three Lee brothers. It resulted in a legendary scorebook entry during Middlesex's first innings when H.W. Lee was caught by F.S. Lee off the bowling of J.W. Lee. However the batsman had made 82 and probably felt he came out ahead. Then, in June 1939, the match between Sussex and Warwickshire included three pairs of brothers – James and John Langridge, Jim and Harry Parks, and Charles and Jack Oates – all of whom were in the Sussex side. Also on the team were 'Tich' and Jim Cornford although, unfortunately for this story, they were not related.

Quite a few fathers and sons have played Test cricket, although not at the same time. Examples from recent times include Chris and Stuart Broad, Walter and Richard Hadlee, Vinoo and Sanjay Manjrekar, and Colin and Chris Cowdrey, both of whom captained England. There are even examples of three generations playing Test cricket. George Headley, known as the 'Black Bradman', his son Ron and his grandson Dean did so, an oddity being that while George and Ron played for the West Indies, Dean played for England. Jahangir Khan played Test cricket for India and, after the partition of India in 1947, his son Majid and grandson Bazid represented Pakistan. It is tempting to include the Parks family here: grandfather Jim and son – also Jim – played for England. Grandson Bobby, who came close to a full Test cap but never received one, also deserves a mention for racing on to the pitch during a Lord's Test to act as substitute wicket-keeper for a while.

Fathers and sons have played in the same county team a number of times giving rise to some unusual scenarios. In July 1931, right at the end of his career, the great old Nottinghamshire cricketer George Gunn, aged 52, scored 183 while opening the batting against Warwickshire. Batting at number eight was his son, George Jr., who scored 100 not out; this is the only time father and son have scored centuries in the same innings. It was a high-scoring draw, both sides only batted once, and it looks like George Jr. was fed a few to make sure he got his ton.

In 1922, there was a relatively near miss at Derby. Willie Quaife, aged 50, and his son Bernard were playing for Warwickshire against Derbyshire. Willie, a former Test player, duly scored a century, but Bernard couldn't do better than 20. In the same match, extraordinarily, Derbyshire were fielding their own father-and-son pairing, Billy and Robert Bestwick. During the game the Bestwicks bowled six overs against the Quaifes, again the only time that has happened. Robert even got Willie out. And if it doesn't confuse the issue too much, it is worth mentioning that the brothers Jack and Cyril Smart were also in the Warwickshire side and Billy Bestwick dismissed them both. Cyril was in at number ten but by 1935 he was batting well enough to hit a then world record of 32 off an over.

Players no longer play into their 50s, so father and sons in the same side don't crop up any more, although in 1991 Alan Butcher and his son Mark both played for Surrey in a one-day game, even if Alan's involvement was largely due to manpower shortage. Sometimes, though, the family cricketing talent does not run deep enough. W.G.'s son, W.G. Jr., failed twice in an Oxford-Cambridge match in the 1890s, reducing his mother to tears.

THERE'S OUT AND THERE'S OUCH

In the 1976 series against the West Indies, played in the Caribbean, India began the fourth Test full of confidence. They had just won the

third Test to level the series at 1-1, making a then record score of 406 for four in the fourth innings. But they left the next Test in Kingston, Jamaica, literally in pieces and in the unusual situation of losing only five wickets in their second innings but being technically all out.

The trouble began in the first innings. It wasn't the West Indies' absolutely all-time top quartet of fast bowlers, but a foursome of Holding, Daniel, Julien and Holder wasn't bad, and they were bowling in the pre-helmet days. West Indies won the toss and, sensing a lively pitch, put India in. During India's first innings, Viswanath broke a finger when caught off Holding; Gaekwad retired hurt after being hit on the left ear and was hospitalised for two days; and Patel, who was hit in the mouth and required stitches, also retired hurt. After a wicket fell to make India 306 for six, the Indian captain, Bishen Bedi, declared. It was no doubt coincidental that he was the next man in.

India's pace attack was much gentler and West Indies took a first innings lead of 85. With Viswanath, Gaekwad and Patel hors de combat, India were three down before they even began their second innings. Madan Lal, normally a number seven, batted at four and Venkataraghavan, subsequently a highly respected umpire but with a Test batting average of only 11, batted at five. After five wickets had fallen, Bedi and Chandresekar reported they had suffered hand injuries while fielding and were unfit to bat. India were all out for 97, leaving West Indies a nominal 13 to win and take the series 2-1. The bottom half of India's scorecard for the second innings made bizarre reading:

AD GAEKWAD	absent hurt
GR VISWANATH	absent hurt
BP PATEL	absent hurt
BS BEDI	absent hurt
BS CHANDRESEKAR	absent hurt

One more oddity is worth mentioning. During the match all 17 members of India's touring party fielded and one of them, Amarnath, ended up in hospital for an appendix operation.

Hit around The Parks

A first-class debut to forget

The Oxford UCCE game against Gloucestershire held in The Parks, Oxford, in April 2005 was an early season warm-up match for the first-class county. A UCCE team is made up of students from the local universities, in this case Oxford and Oxford Brookes. Such games are often a mismatch, as recently exemplified by the game in April 2012 between Durham and Durham MCCU (as UCCEs are now called), when the undergraduates were all out for 18 in their second innings, one of the lowest totals ever.

For the county, the result of these matches is often secondary to gaining some good batting practice – that is why Gloucestershire chose not to make the undergraduates follow on, even with a first-innings lead of 189. With an over to go at the end of the second day, Gloucestershire

were on 228 for one, having scored at almost 5 runs an over. Facing the last over was their opening batsman, Craig Spearman, on 136. Spearman somewhat outclassed the young players up against him: he was a very hard-hitting, aggressive batsman who had played 19 Tests for New Zealand. It was therefore probably a bit unfair of the Oxford UCCE captain Luke Parker to toss the ball to Stephen Moreton for this last over. Moreton was a leg break bowler, not a genus known for economy. And he was no doubt nervous because this would be his first over in first-class cricket.

Spearman licked his lips and told the wicket-keeper he was going to hit every ball out of the ground. He almost did, hitting Moreton for 6, 6, 6, 6, 4 and 6, a total of 34 runs, the third highest number of runs ever hit off one over. In fairness to Moreton, it should be said that Spearman was dropped twice but, just the same, he has gone into the record books as the bowler of the most expensive debut over in first-class cricket. Next morning Spearman, on 170 overnight, took his score to 216 made off only 168 balls before retiring out. Oxford, after being 24 for six in their second innings, hung on to salvage a one-sided draw.

Who got the runs?

When the B's took on the rest, and other strange games

Outside the serious business of organised cricket in championships and leagues, people desperate for a game turn to informal, knock-up matches. An early example of such a game is described in shopkeeper Thomas Turner's diary for 19 May 1760, where he says 'This day was played in the park a cricket match between an eleven whose names were John in this parish and an eleven of any other name, which I suppose was won by the latter with ease.'

The cricket historian H.T. Waghorn (1842-1930) recorded many more bizarre match examples. In a famous game in 1766, 11 one-armed men played 11 one-legged men, all pensioners of Greenwich Hospital. The match was played at Blackheath and several thousand spectators attended. 'The one-legged men played best,' Waghorn says, 'but the one-

armed men ran best, by which means, after a long and difficult contest, victory was declared for the one-armed heroes.' Similar games were played in 1796 and 1863.

Again in 1766, 11 poulterers and 11 butchers of Leadenhall Market played 'for a considerable sum of money and a fine whole lamb for supper.' Waghorn also recounts a single-wicket game 'between a person with a wooden leg, and a young man with a half hundred weight slung on his back,' and says that 'after the most laborious exertions on both sides [the contest] was decided in favour of the man loaded with the weight.'

In 1768, Waghorn reported that a match took place between 11 married and 11 single women 'for a plum cake and a barrel of ale' – the single women won that. In 1784, he also tells us that the married men of Titchbourne Down near Alresford, Hampshire, played the bachelors for 25 guineas, a game the married men won 'after a severe contest for upwards of nine hours.'

Other offbeat games include two contests between Smokers and Non-Smokers at Lord's in 1884 and in Melbourne in 1887. The games had first-class status, and great names such as W.G. and E.M. Grace, Fred Spofforth, Lord Harris, George Giffen and Dick Barlow took part. The Non-Smokers won the first match and the second was drawn – the Ashes were not at stake in either.

In 2006 and 2011, teams of transplant recipients representing Great Britain and Australia competed for the David Hookes Memorial Shield – Australia won on both occasions. David Hookes was an Australian Test cricketer and an organ donor. When he died in 2004, ten people received his transplanted organs.

Admiral Jellicoe, who commanded the British fleet at the Battle of Jutland in 1916, took a team of admirals to play the Nautical College at Pangbourne in 1928. The cadets batted first and made 117. After early losses, the admirals rallied and passed their total although Jellicoe was sunk on the fifth ball for a duck.

There are reports of at least two games on horseback during the eighteenth century. Left-handers have played right-handers, and a team beginning with B has played the Rest of England. In *Bats, Balls and Bails*, Les Scott mentions a game between Flatulents and Constipators although he doesn't say who, if anyone, got the runs.

A perfect over

Then Gibbs gives it away

One of a batsman's 'Holy Grails' is to hit every ball in a six-ball over for six. No one has done so in Test cricket and only four players have done so in first-class and List A (one-day) cricket. Gary Sobers was the first to do this, playing for Nottinghamshire in a county game in 1968, off the bowling of Glamorgan's Malcolm Nash. Ravi Shastri then did so for Bombay against Baroda in 1985, off the bowling of Tilak Raj.

South African batsman Herschelle Gibbs was the first to do so in an ODI, playing in the 2007 World Cup, off the bowling of Daan van Bunge in a game against the Netherlands. In his autobiography *To The Point*, Gibbs gives a shot-by-shot account of the over. He describes what it's like to be 'in the zone' with an uncanny feeling for where the bowler is going to bowl.

He also says that he was unaware at the time that a sponsor had put up a $1 million prize for the first person to manage this – however his teammates knew. The South Africa team had a rule that whoever won a money prize kept 50 per cent, with the rest split amongst the rest of the team. So while his teammates were pleased for Gibbs, they were also busily calculating their share.

Unfortunately for them, it didn't turn out quite as they had imagined. The sponsor's rules were that the prize money had to be donated to a charity, and Gibbs chose Habitat for Humanity with projects in Trinidad and Johannesburg. However he was allowed to retain another reward – honorary citizenship of St Kitts and Nevis, apparently valued at $300,000. He later spent his honeymoon there.

The fourth of the players to achieve this feat had much better luck. Yuvraj Singh hit Chris Broad of England for six sixes later the same year in a game played in Durban during the Twenty20 World Cup Tournament. He received Rs10 million ($252,700) and also won a Porsche. However, the final feel-good factor must surely belong to Gibbs.

Snowballs in June
The dentally challenged batsman

On Monday 2 June 1975, the second day of a three-day game between Derbyshire and Lancashire at Buxton, the players set off from home to travel to the game in sunshine. However, by the time they arrived at the cricket ground it was under a few inches of snow. Buxton was the highest altitude ground in the country and weather could be changeable, even in June.

The umpire Dickie Bird was fond of recalling the circumstances: 'When I went out to inspect the wicket, the snow was level with the top of my

boots. I'd never seen anything like it!' Lancashire players Clive Lloyd and Farokh Engineer, from West Indies and India respectively, didn't see much snow where they came from and enjoyed lobbing snowballs at each other in the outfield. For the first time ever, snow caused play to be abandoned for the day.

Everyone thought that the final day of the match, Tuesday, would be a write-off, too. Yet it turned out to be lovely and Dickie Bird got the game under way again. Lancashire had enjoyed excellent batting conditions on the first day, making 477 for five, but now the pitch turned spiteful and the Lancashire fast bowlers Peter Lever and Peter Lee enjoyed themselves as balls reared off a length. The Derbyshire batsmen couldn't cope and wickets fell quickly.

The number five batsman in particular, Ashley Harvey-Walker, didn't like the look of it. He was so sure his innings would be brief that when he arrived at the wicket he took out his false teeth, handing them to Dickie Bird. Bird explained afterwards: 'He wrapped them in a handkerchief and asked me to look after them. He said not to worry because he wouldn't be in for long. I'm glad to say he collected his teeth two overs later.' Derbyshire were all out for 42 in the first innings and 87 in the second. The combination of the snow and Harvey-Walker's false teeth had made it a memorable match.

Harvey-Walker never became a regular in the Derbyshire side and his first-class career ended only three years later. Eventually he moved to Johannesburg where he became an assistant groundsman and the part owner of a bar. He was drinking there one day in 1997 when a man came into the bar and called out his name. When Harvey-Walker identified himself, the man took out a gun and shot the former cricketer dead, making him only the second first-class English player to be murdered. To this day, the murder remains unsolved.

THE LONG AND THE SHORT OF IT

He was a hard-hitting batsman who played first-class cricket for Fiji between 1947-48 and 1953-54. He was an adequate rather than outstanding number three, with an average of 41.29. And as Fiji played very little first-class cricket, his career consisted of only nine games.

However, he holds one world record that may never be beaten: he has the longest name of anyone who has played first-class cricket: Ilikena Lazarus Talebulamainavaleniveivakabulaimainakulalakebalau, a total of 63 letters. The translation of his name resembles a potted biography: 'Returned alive from Nankuka hospital at Lakemba island in the Lau group.' To grateful scorers he is known simply as I.L. Bula. A scorecard entry for Andhra v. Kerala, a Ranji Trophy game in India in 1990, runs him close: Chamundeswaranath c. Balasubramaniam b. Ananthapadmanabhan – all that for 2.

Like many Fijian players, Bula was an exuberant fielder. On one occasion, playing against Canterbury in 1948, he dropped a difficult catch in the outfield. Later he missed another hard one and, although barefooted, expressed his disgust by punting the ball from long on back to the bowler. But another even more difficult chance came his way. He caught it and in his delight threw the ball from long on to the fence behind the third man, probably not less than a distance of 100yds (91m). One of his compatriots, Petero Kubunavanua, who fielded in a **sulu**, ***the Fijian skirt-like garment, was so admired for his fielding and bullet-like throws that he was shown on the stamps issued to celebrate the centenary of cricket in Fiji.***

Neither home nor away

The short, odd, first-class career of Harry Wilson

One of cricket's great joys is the oddities it throws up in even the shortest of careers – and you couldn't have had one that was much shorter or odder than H. (Harry) Wilson's. He played only one game in first-class cricket; it was for Northamptonshire at Peterborough in 1931 against the New Zealand touring team. Primarily a medium pace bowler, he batted at number 11 in each innings. His career record was: Matches, 1; Innings, 2; Not out, 0; Highest score, 0; Average, 0.00. He could only have batted for the shortest of periods. Even so, he managed to achieve a bizarre double.

In the first innings he was run out without facing a ball – so far, so bad. Came the second innings – and exactly the same thing happened. Another oddity is that although nominally Northamptonshire were playing at home, Peterborough is in fact in Cambridgeshire. Wilson's entire career arguably took place in no man's land, neither home nor away. Let us not leave him totally without achievement: he bowled in both innings. In the first, he was economical although he didn't take a wicket. However, the highlight of his first-class career came with New Zealand on 125 for three in the second innings, when he took the wicket of Page. New Zealand made the winning runs shortly afterwards, so he got his entry in the scorebook just in time.

One person who ran Wilson's record close was Frederick Hyland, who was selected to play for Hampshire against Northamptonshire in 1924. The Hampshire eleven was very strong and contained Lord Tennyson, Mead, Kennedy, Brown, Livesey and Newman. Hyland squeezed in at 11, but it mattered not. Only two overs of play were possible in the whole match and only 1 run was scored. The playing time could not have amounted to more than five or six minutes. Like Wilson, Hyland was never selected again, although those five minutes entitled him to an obituary in *Wisden*.

You might have thought that Hyland's performance would not

have attracted much attention except to collectors of cricket trivia, but the sheer absurdity of the situation inspired the cricket writer, Ronald Mason. In his book, *Sing All a Green Willow*, he wrote an excellent essay entitled *Of the Late Frederick J. Hyland* that described the glory of having played first-class cricket, for however brief a spell, and despite lack of achievement.

PUTTING A BACKSPIN ON IT

The Middlesex slow left-armer, Jack Young, was one of the team's most successful pre- and post-Second World War bowlers. However, of his almost 1,200 first-class wickets, one dismissal must rank as one of the strangest ever.

In August 1948, Middlesex were playing Warwickshire in a county game at Lord's. On the Warwickshire side was the New Zealander, Martin Donnelly. Donnelly, aged 32, was a very gifted all-round sportsman who had played Test cricket for New Zealand before the War at the age of only 19, and rugby for England in 1947. He had just been selected as one of* Wisden's *Five Cricketers of the Year.

Donnelly had been stumped off Young for 35 in the first innings. In the second, he was going well on 55 when a ball from Young hit him on the foot, bounced high over his head and the wicket, and landed behind the stumps. Terrific backspin then caused the ball to spin back towards the wicket and dislodge the bails. Donnelly was out bowled – probably the only man to have been bowled from behind the stumps. He played against Young the following year in a Test at Lord's and was out to him again but in a more orthodox fashion, being caught by Hutton, and not before he had made a brilliant 206.

Jammy for the Jam Sahib

Ranji's legendary record

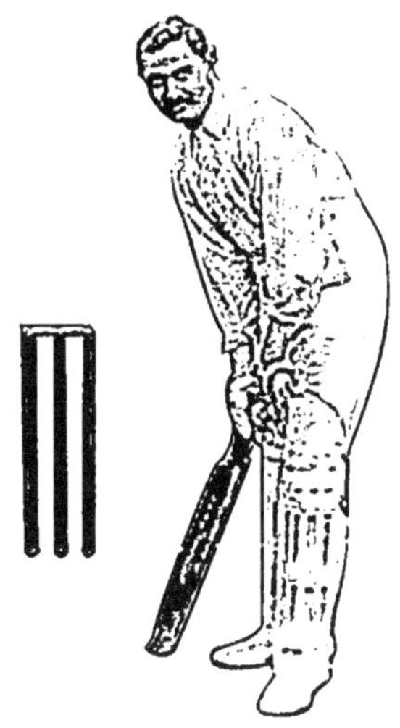

Ranjitsinhji Vibhaji, Maharaja Jam Sahib of Nawanagarber, is known to cricketing posterity as 'Ranji'. He was the first Indian to play Test cricket, albeit for England. An outstanding batsman, his style drew the most extravagant praise from his peers such as W.G. Grace, and one of his feats remains unbeaten to this day.

He was playing for Sussex against Yorkshire at Hove in 1896, a three-day game. By the end of day two, Sussex were faltering. Ranji had just come into bat and was 0 not out. The next morning he took his score to 100 out of a Sussex innings of 190 all out before being caught. Sussex were made to follow on and in due course Ranji batted again. In his second innings on the same day, he scored 125 not out and Sussex saved the game. It is the only time in first-class cricket history that a batsman has made two centuries on the same day. Even so, it didn't do much for Sussex's season: they finished bottom while Yorkshire won the Championship.

Another exploit attributed to Ranji sounds even more unlikely, and possibly is. In August 1892, whilst a student at Cambridge, he is said to have played in three games in one day and scored a century in each. After scoring 128 in his first innings, he wandered off to look at other games while his side continued its innings. He found a team that was a man short and accepted their invitation to bat for them, scoring 132 before returning to his first side. As they were still batting, he wandered off yet again, joined in another game, and inevitably scored another hundred, this time 150.

According to Simon Wilde in *Ranji: The Strange Genius of Ranjitsinhji*, the truth is more likely to be a combination of two different stories. In August 1892 he certainly did play for three different teams and scored centuries for each, but that was over a period of six days. It is also true that he played for two different teams on the same day whilst at Cambridge. The two stories appear to have become irresistibly merged and have now become part of the Ranji legend.

All over in four and a half hours

The lowest-scoring match on record

It was a first-class game scheduled to take place over three days in May 1878 between the MCC and the Australian touring team at Lord's. In fact the game, described by W.G. Grace as 'one of the most remarkable and sensational ever played at Lord's', was over in four and a half hours.

Wet weather, followed by baking sunshine, had made the wicket 'almost unplayable' according to W.G. The MCC, who had won the toss and chosen to bat, were 27 for three at one stage in their first innings, with Grace out for 4. Then Fred Spofforth, the Australian fast bowler, took six for four and MCC were all out for 33 in 65 minutes. In the difficult batting conditions, the Australians did not do much better. The England bowler Alfred Shaw bowled 46 deliveries before a run was scored off him. After being 23 for eight, the Australians managed to reach 41 off 66 (4-ball) overs.

The 8 run difference on first innings was not great and MCC were in with a fair chance if they only batted reasonably well. They did not; the progression of their second innings was painful. They were 0 for two, with Grace out bowled by Spofforth; 1 for four; 16 for five. Their last five wickets went down for 2 runs and they were all out for 19. A contemporary report says that Spofforth was so delighted at bowling Grace that 'he jumped about two feet in the air, and sang out: "Bowled! Bowled! Bowled!"' And at the finish in the dressing room, he said: 'Ain't I a

demon? Ain't I a demon?' Spofforth's match figures were ten for 20 and thereafter he was known as 'Demon' Spofforth. Requiring 12 to win, the Australians made them for the loss of one wicket, although it took them 16 overs to do so.

Two strong teams had scored a grand total of 105 runs in a completed game, still a record low aggregate in a match where a team has bowled out its opponents twice. W.G. had experienced something similar at least once before. In 1872, playing for MCC against Surrey, his side batted first and were an astonishing 0 for seven and 2 for eight, eventually reaching 16. At one stage the scoreboard showed the unlikely details of 8 runs, nine wickets, last man eight. This game was also over in one day, not counting the first day which had been rained off, with Surrey, requiring 39, winning by five wickets.

UMPIRE, PLAYER, UMPIRE

In English cricket in particular, more often than not umpires are drawn from the ranks of retired cricketers. It is a pleasant way for them to stay in the game and they are familiar with all its little tricks. However, on the basis that – like Caesar's wife – they should be 'above suspicion', for a long time they were not permitted to stand in games involving their old county. This is very different to the experience of the Australian George Coulthard in the 1880s. He was both umpire and player, virtually

simultaneously, at international level.

Coulthard was born in 1856 and excelled at both cricket and Aussie rules football. By the time he was 20 he was playing football for Carlton, winning a championship medal the following year. Changing sports, a couple of years later in 1879 he was involved in the one-off Test between England and Australia, although not as a player but as an umpire, at the remarkably young age of 22. He had a close-up view as 'Demon' Spofforth took the first ever Test hat-trick.

Coulthard must have had a penchant for umpiring because the following year he umpired an important Aussie rules football match. He was still active in both sports and in February 1882 was again involved in a Test, this time as a player. Played as a bowler, he never got to bowl and in his one innings scored 6 not out. He was never selected again so reverted to umpiring and no one seemed to mind that he stood in the fourth Test a month later.

Coulthard was active at the dawn of the Test cricket era and had the kind of career that you cannot imagine happening today. However in those days the infrastructure wasn't anything like so well developed and perhaps what happened to him did not seem nearly so strange at the time. Who knows what further twists and turns his career might have taken, but he died of consumption aged only 27.

Five of the best
The cricketer who should have read Wisden

Each year, following a tradition dating back to 1889, *Wisden* publishes its Cricketers of the Year based on performances in the previous season. Selection is one of the greatest honours in cricket, and players with a chance of selection no doubt eagerly await the announcement. However, due to an unlikely set of circumstances, one of the five chosen names in 1918 didn't receive the news that he'd been selected until the 1990s. What is more, he had never played first-class cricket!

During the First World War there was no first-class cricket, and there were no *Wisden* choices in 1916 and 1917. For the 1918 edition, based on performances in the 1917 season, the editor decided to choose five School Bowlers of the Year, one of them being Harry Calder. They were prescient choices as all of them went on to play first-class cricket, except – uniquely among *Wisden* Cricketers of the Year – Calder. One of them, Stevens, went on to play for England ten times and to captain them on one occasion.

Yet the South African-born Calder never got beyond playing once for Surrey Second XI in 1920 without distinguishing himself. He returned to South Africa with his family and was lost to history until he was tracked down by the cricket historian Robert Brooke in 1994. It was only then, at the age of 93, that he discovered that he had been one of *Wisden's* Five Cricketers of the Year 76 years earlier.

He insisted that he was not aware of the honour until Brooke told him, although it seems strange that he lived and played cricket in England until at least 1920 and no one mentioned it.

The annual number of cricketers selected has been five since 1891, except on four occasions. In 1896, 1921 and 1926 only one was selected to pay special honour to W.G. Grace, Sir Pelham Warner and Sir Jack Hobbs respectively. The fourth occasion, in 1913, saw the selection of John Wisden himself who, having died in 1884, was posthumously honoured.

In 2011 – very unusually – only four names were announced. A fifth had been selected, generally reported to be the Pakistani pace bowler Mohammad Amir. However he was involved in the 2010 spot-fixing scandal and although at the time the criminal trial had not taken place, the *Wisden* editor, Scyld Berry, felt it would be inappropriate to include him. Amir was subsequently found guilty and sentenced to six months' imprisonment. The International Cricket Council (ICC) also banned him from playing for five years.

A *Wisden* rule is that you can only be chosen once although it has been broken on two occasions – for Warner and Hobbs. The early editions had a good proportion of almanack to supplement the cricket. The first edition contained a monthly calendar, a list of the major Civil War battles, an account of the trial of Charles I and the rules of quoiting; the important stuff about cricket didn't begin until page 13.

CLUBS WITH NO HOMES

Wandering or nomadic teams – cricket clubs with no ground of their own that play all their games away – have a long and honourable history dating back to the middle of the nineteenth century. Perhaps two of the best known are I Zingari, with its distinctive black, red and gold club colours, and Free Foresters. These clubs have names that tend to the unusual, such as the Devon Dumplings or the Stragglers of Asia. To play for the latter you originally had to have lived east of Suez for at least two years.

Some wandering clubs have a

USP (Unique Selling Point), like the XL Club whose membership is restricted to those over 35 (it used to be 40, hence the name). Another club, the Wiltshire Queries, founded in the early 1930s, decided they would not have a written Constitution. However, when they tried to open an account with the Post Office, they were told they must produce a list of rules. A one-line constitution was hastily written on the back of an envelope there and then: 'No person suffering from persistent boils on the neck shall be eligible for membership', and this was found acceptable.

Challenging any wandering team for eccentricity is the Fellowship of Fairly Odd Places Cricket Club (FFOP CC). Formed in 2005 by Dutch cricket lovers, they play only once a year but their venues are memorably unusual. They have played in two countries at once when their cricket ground straddled the

Holland-Belgium border; in 2008 they challenged the Vatican in Rome and played in the Stadio dei Marmi amongst 60 marble statues; they have played against Iceland; and they have played on an uninhabited island. They are now planning to play in Andorra on the highest pitch in Europe – the first cricket game in the principality's history – in the presence of the Head of State.

Out twice before Lynch

Monte's terrible morning

Surrey batsman Monte Lynch was a popular, hard-hitting middle-order batsman who played first-class cricket for 20 years, scored over 18,000 runs at a reasonable average, and played three times for England in ODIs. So he was nobody's rabbit. However a set of circumstances arose during a game between Middlesex and Surrey that earned him a unique and unwanted distinction. You could scratch your head for quite a while before working out how Lynch managed to get out twice before lunch in a county game, both times for a duck.

At the start of August 1977, the County Championship was a three-way race between Middlesex, Kent and Gloucestershire. Middlesex were due to play Lynch's team, Surrey, at Lord's on Saturday, Monday and Tuesday of August 6, 8 and 9. Saturday, the first day, was totally washed out by rain. On Monday, Middlesex won the toss and put Surrey in, but only five overs' play were possible with Surrey ending on 8 for one.

So when the game restarted on Tuesday, the draw was the obvious option with both sides trying for maximum bonus points. However although the weather was dry the pitch, which had remained uncovered, was green, damp and perfectly suited to the faster bowlers. The Middlesex opening bowlers, Daniel and Selvey, destroyed the Surrey batsmen in little over an hour – among them Monte Lynch, batting at three, caught behind for a duck.

Now it was Middlesex's turn. It was expected that they would try to reach a score of 300 and get four valuable batting points to add to the four bowling points they had already gained. It was therefore a surprise when Middlesex opened the batting with two of the lower-order players; even more of a surprise when one of them, John Emburey, had a swish at the first ball and then marched back to the pavilion. The Middlesex skipper Mike Brearley, in his first season as England captain, had sniffed an unlikely victory worth 12 Championship points on the bowler-friendly pitch and declared as soon as his side had faced the one ball needed to make it a valid innings.

Surrey had to bat again before lunch in the same difficult conditions in which they had just failed. Monte Lynch was soon in again and just as soon out, this time bowled. For the second time in the morning he had failed to trouble the scorers. Two ducks before lunch was unique; the Surrey batsman Geoff Howarth, the New Zealand Test player, was also out twice before lunch – but at least he scored on both occasions.

Surrey batted only a little better second time around and were all out for 89; this left Middlesex needing 139 to win. In a race against the clock, they got there with an over or two to spare, winning by nine wickets. Imaginative captaincy had maximised Middlesex's points, but at the end of the season it was not quite enough – Middlesex and Kent finished joint champions.

The nearest challenger to Lynch for speedy dismissals appears to be the Pakistani Test player, Ebbu Ghazali. Playing against England at Old Trafford in 1954, he was twice out for a duck within two hours, the fastest pair in Test history. Bad weather meant Pakistan saved the Test, but it was Ghazali's last Test match. Not far behind is the Australian Test batsman, Neil Harvey. He was out twice in an afternoon to Jim Laker in the 1956 Old Trafford Ashes Test when Laker took 19 Australian wickets. Harvey, one of Australia's greatest post-War Test players, lasted a grand total of three balls.

STRAIGHT TO THE CORE

From time to time an umpire's authority and sense of humour is tested by a player's high jinks. In 1972, when Sussex played Australia in a rain-affected one-day game at Hove, the renowned Australian fast bowler Dennis Lillee tells in his book My Life in Cricket how he brought an apple with him after the lunch break and bowled it at a Sussex batsman. The apple split in two on hitting the pitch, one half hitting the batsman plumb lbw and the other half bowling him. As Lillee prepared to appeal, the alert umpire quick-wittedly flung out his arm and instead of 'no-ball' shouted 'no apple!'

Rippon – or rip-off?

When the tax people looked the other way

It must have been a puzzling experience for the home spectators at the Somerset v. Gloucestershire game played at Taunton in June 1919. Gloucestershire had batted first and made 283. When Somerset batted, they were soon in trouble at 25 for three. However the number four batsman was batting well, taking part in productive stands, which steadied the innings. Referring to the scorecard, spectators learned that he was S. Trimnell, a new name to them.

His was certainly a very promising debut, even if something seemed a little odd. Trimnell bore a remarkable resemblance to the Somerset batsman, A.D.E. (Dudley) Rippon, who had opened the innings and made 0. The scarcely believable thought crossed their minds: Dudley hadn't batted again under an assumed name, had he? This would be totally against the rules, of course. The only other possibility was even stranger. Dudley did have an identical twin called Sydney who frequently played for Somerset alongside Dudley; but if it was Sidney, why on earth was he batting under the name of S. Trimnell?

The spectators were right – a scam was indeed going on and it didn't take much time for it to unravel. In the first season after the end of the First World War Somerset, like many counties, were under financial pressure and relied heavily on amateurs such as the Rippons to make up the team. But not all amateurs had large private incomes that left them free to play county cricket whenever they wished. In fact Sydney had a job in the Inland Revenue, which occasionally allowed him time off to play, although not on this occasion. Sydney decided to report in sick and play anyway. Needing a cover, he chose his grandmother's name, Trimnell.

However making 92 in the first innings – his highest career score to that point – and 58 not out in the second, was overdoing it and the cause of his unmasking. People immediately wanted to know more about this unknown batting sensation and London newspapers sent in requests for further information. Since a large number of people connected with Somerset now knew who he was, Sydney had little option but to come clean and throw himself on the mercy of the Inland Revenue.

Perhaps the employment rules were a little less strict for returning servicemen for there were no repercussions. In fact, he did so well in the tax office that a little over two years later he was made an Inspector of Taxes. There can't be many of them who have played first-class cricket, which he continued to do until he retired in 1929. He returned to playing in 1937 but by then he was 45, well past his prime and not very successful. One of his children was Geoffrey Rippon, a cabinet minister in the Ted Heath government (1970-74).

There are no other known instances of cricketers playing under an assumed identity, although players not looking themselves on the cricket field is not uncommon.

THREE CLAIMS TO FAME

Andy Ducat (1886–1942) has a place in cricket history for three reasons – athletic, farcical and tragic by turn. Athletic is justified because Ducat is one of that very elite group of a dozen English sportsmen who have represented their country at cricket and soccer. He played once for England at cricket and six times at football; he also captained Aston Villa to their sixth FA Cup win in the 1919–20 season. Others among the exclusive group include C.B. Fry, Tip Foster (the only man to captain his country at both sports), Arthur Milton and Willie Watson.

Farcical comes from Ducat's extraordinary experience in 1921 while batting in his only Test. Playing a shot against the Australian fast bowler Ted McDonald, the shoulder of his bat broke. The ball flew off to slip where it was caught. Meanwhile the splinter from his bat ricocheted on to his stumps, meaning he was also out hit wicket. Both were legitimate dismissals and either could have been entered in the scorebook. The scorer settled for caught.

Tragic results from the manner of Ducat's death. Aged 56, he was playing for Surrey Home Guard at Lord's against Sussex Home Guard in July 1942. On the first day of the match, he came into bat at number five and began to compile a steady innings. With his score at 29, he played a ball to mid-on and then collapsed on to the pitch. Although those around him did their best, he could not be revived. The game was promptly abandoned. He is the only person ever to have died at Lord's while actually playing.

Reaping the benefit

How Dickie Dodds batted for God

One of the most entertaining and dashing players of the immediate post-War era was Dickie Dodds, an opening batsman for Essex from 1946 to 1959. You knew you would always get good entertainment from a Dodds innings, if it went on long enough. What you might not have known was that his free and aggressive batting was an expression of his faith that was based upon the religious and moral movement, Moral Re-Armament (MRA). He believed that lovely strokes gave pleasure to God and if he got out whilst attempting them, so be it. To him, his innings were the cricketing equivalent of building a cathedral, both being dedicated to the greater glory of God.

His creed was put under a severe test in 1957 when, after 11 years of county service, Dodds applied for and was granted a benefit match. A benefit was particularly valuable to a cricketer of Dodds's era: it was tax-free and one of the few perks that cricketers received. Dodds discussed dates and matches with the county secretary. He was disappointed to find that his options at the main ground, Chelmsford, were fewer than expected. One by one the county, that naturally wanted to keep the proceeds from those games for itself, ruled out the most attractive fixtures, such as the Bank Holiday game.

Dodds became quite angry; as he says in his autobiography *Hit Hard and Enjoy It*, 'I thought I had served the county well and should have been given the game of my choice.' Referring the problem to God, Dodds felt rebuked by the response: 'You are on the get; your club is on the get; the whole country is on the get. You all need to live on the give. Make your benefit a demonstration of being on the give.'

Dodds took a new approach instead. He realised that for the first time in many years two matches were scheduled to take place in Leyton, in London's East End. He had a number of friends there and he felt more at home there than in Chelmsford. Of the two games, the weekend match was one of those already ruled out by the county, so that left him with the mid-week game against Middlesex. There were some drawbacks, but among the advantages were that Middlesex was a neighbouring county with a strong, attractive side which might even include the iconic England batsman, Denis Compton, thereby drawing a good crowd.

It was at this point that Dodds took a gigantic and possibly unique gamble, although he would not have thought of it like that. Beneficiaries were entitled to the proceeds of the gate money from the game but had to cover the outgoing costs themselves. In theory, if the match was rained off, they could make a loss as there would be no income but they would still have to pay the expenses. Usually the beneficiary insured against the risk; Dodds took the problem to God. He said that the answer he received was: 'If I want you to have the money – I will give you the weather.' So he decided not to insure against rain. Although his teammates were astonished, he received support from one or two unexpected places such as the blunt-spoken England fast bowler, Freddie Trueman.

The benefit match produced excellent cricket, although not without one or two twinges of anxiety for Dodds. Essex, batting first, were shot out for 115 on 'a typical Essex seamer's wicket'. It looked like Dodds's own groundsman wasn't on his side. However, Denis Compton was indeed in the Middlesex side and not out overnight on the first day. His presence drew a large second day crowd, which knew that the talismanic batsman's career was coming to a close. Compton responded with a century before lunch, his last but one hundred in first-class cricket. Essex, batting much better in their second innings, set Middlesex 219 to win and managed to bowl them out on the stroke of time to win the game.

And the weather? It was 'the finest of the summer,' Dodds recorded. 'Three perfect, sunny days.' The crowds were large with good gate receipts and 'record collections for the beneficiary', producing a £2,325 surplus for Dodds. True to his principles, he turned the whole amount over to MRA.

THE TWO MILLIONTH RUN

When Sri Lanka played England at Colombo in April 2012, a four by Thilan Samaraweera brought up the two millionth run in Test cricket. It was hard to know whether this was more or less than you'd have guessed, especially when it sometimes seems that Sachin Tendulkar has scored two million runs on his own.

The highest aggregate in a game is the 1,981 runs scored in the Timeless Test in Durban between South Africa and England in March 1939, a match that lasted for nine days spread over 12 days. The match still ended in a draw with England on 654 for five, needing only 42 to win but having to catch the boat home.

Ignoring one rain-affected Test, the lowest aggregate in a completed game is 291 when England played Australia at Lord's in 1888. Australia won by 61 runs and their 116 in the first innings was the only total over 100. The highest individual score of the match was W.G. Grace's 24 in England's second innings.

The batsman who contributed most to the two million is Sachin

Tendulkar with 15,470 runs and 51 centuries. Sir Donald Bradman has the best average per innings with 99.94 and also the highest number of runs in a series with 974. The West Indian, Brian Lara, has the highest individual innings with 400 not out scored in Antigua against England in April 2004; his 28 hit off Robin Peterson is the highest number of runs scored off one over.

And the three millionth run? If the average number of runs scored per Test remains at about 1,000 and the 45 to 50 Tests played per year stay the same, that will be reached in about 2024.

In your own words
Choice entries in the scorebook

There are ten 'canonical' ways of being dismissed in cricket, such as bowled, caught, lbw and so on, and the scorer duly enters these in the scorebook. Beyond that, a batsman occasionally retires 'hurt', or for other reasons which the scorer can record pretty much as takes his or her fancy.

For example in the eighteenth century, according to a New Zealand newspaper, a batsman was recorded out 'P.H.O'. Nobody now knows what it means, although 'put hand out' has been suggested. In the nineteenth century, T. Hills was out 'hat fell on wicket', although today that would be 'hit wicket'. H. Bolsover 'refused to play' and O.C. Pell 'left his wicket thinking he was bowled'. O. Mordaunt 'left his wicket, obliged to go'. If that reference was indeed referring to Osbert Mordaunt (1842-1923), possibly he was obliged to go because he was a Canon and should have been in church, not playing cricket.

In 1995 Robin Wightman of Whiteleas CC, in the middle of a very successful bowling spell, objected to being taken off and replaced by his captain, stomping off the field in protest. His absence was recorded 'out huffed'. In 1879, T.A. Fison scored 264 not out for Hendon against Highgate School and ran every run. He then left the game and his exit was recorded as 'retired to catch train to continent'. Other batsmen have been recorded as 'ran away, scared by bowler', 'dropped spectacles on wicket', 'shamefully refused to go in', 'absent baby-sitting', 'retired hot', 'retired suffering from measles', 'absent frozen' (*see* Cricket in high places…) and 'sick on pitch'. In 1927, the England cricketer Ian Peebles was on tour in South Africa when he slipped away for a dip in the sea during his side's innings. By the time he returned they were all out and the scorers had entered him as 'absent bathing'.

To digress momentarily, 'sick on pitch' is a reminder of the game in 1986 when the Australian Dean Jones was batting against India in a Test at Madras. The heat and humidity were intense and Jones was extremely dehydrated, every so often stopping to vomit (off the wicket, of course, otherwise he would have been in breach of the Laws). His partner was the Australian captain Allan Border, a Queenslander and a real 'hard man'. Jones told him he felt he was too ill to continue. 'If you can't hack it,' Border replied, 'let's get a tough Queenslander out here – get me Greg Ritchie!' Naturally Jones stayed put, going on to make 210 and helping to tie the Test, one of only two ties in Test match history.

In 1870, James Southerton (1827-80) was playing for Surrey against MCC with W.G. Grace in its side. Southerton was not a very good batsman and Grace says that they often used to tease him that he sometimes closed his eyes to hit. It was of this game that Grace writes, 'Once, when I was fielding at point, I proved it by claiming a catch from a ball which had palpably struck the ground before I caught it. "Jimmy" opened his eyes just in time to see me toss up the ball, and I, to carry on the joke, said he had given me a "hot'un"; then he believed he was caught, and walked out. The fieldsmen told him he was not out, and Pooley whistled him to return, but Southerton would not believe it.' That explains the odd entry in the scorebook: 'retired thinking he was out'. Southerton was the oldest man to make his Test debut, aged 49; he was also the first Test cricketer to die.

Two batsmen who died during games had differing entries. Andy Ducat, who died while actually batting (*see* Andy Ducat's three claims to fame), was shown as 'not out', which has a kind of logic. In the first innings of a game in 1959, Abdul Aziz, playing for Karachi, was hit over the heart and collapsed on the pitch; he died on the way to hospital aged only 17. The scorebook entry for the first innings shows 'retired hurt 0' and for the second innings 'absent dead'.

THE HOAX INVITATION

We are so used to the primacy of the England-Australia cricket rivalry that it may come as a surprise to learn that the first ever international game did not involve either side. Involved instead were teams from two countries that are no longer mainstream cricket-playing nations, Canada and the USA.

First contact was at club level, but against a strange background. In 1840 St George's Club, New York, received an invitation from a Mr Philpotts to send a team to play against the Toronto Cricket Club. The team arrived in Toronto only to find that the invitation was a hoax and they were not expected at all. A game was hastily arranged which St George's won by ten wickets, possibly due to good manners from the embarrassed Canadian club.

It was not until September 1844 that the first game with claims to be called an International took place, Canada winning by 23 runs. It looks like the scorers had difficulty identifying all the players since four of the wickets are credited to 'unknown'. A crowd of about 20,000 is said to have attended and bets estimated at around $120,00 were placed, equivalent to about $2 million at today's rates.

This was thought to be the first contest between two countries in any sport of the modern era. There were subsequent games in 1845 and 1846, all won by Canada, and it was not until 1853 that USA won its first game. So why did cricket never become the national sport of either country? Perhaps because the north American temperament couldn't cope with the leisurely pace of a game that can last from three to five days and still end up without a result.

Slowly does it
Nadkarni on the money

Back in the 1950s and 1960s, Test cricket could be a tedious safety-first affair with both sides reluctant to take the initiative and risk losing. In some games fewer than 200 runs a day were scored. Of the ten Test matches with the lowest run rates, eight took place in the 1950s.

Spectacular bowling analyses were recorded during this period. In January 1964, when India played England in Madras, during England's first innings the Indian spinner, Bapu Nadkarni, gave away 5 runs in 32 overs and bowled 131 consecutive dot (scoreless) balls. Apparently he practiced accuracy by bowling at a coin and trying to hit it. Anyway, in this game he was right on the money. When, after 131 deliveries, he was finally nudged for a single, *The Times* reporter commented laconically that he 'was immediately taken off as though being altogether too expensive'.

Nadkarni's feat was not even the most consecutive dot balls bowled in cricket history. That honour belongs to Hugh 'Toey' Tayfield of South Africa in 1957 at Durban, against an England batting line-up containing Compton, May and Cowdrey, three of England's finest post-War batsmen. Bowling eight-ball overs, Tayfield finished his first innings spell with 119 consecutive dot balls, followed by a further 18 in the second innings. He thus bowled 137 consecutive dot balls, still a record – thank goodness, one might add.

Parsimonious bowling also requires strokeless batsmen. The record in Tests is held by the New Zealand number 11, Geoff Allott, who faced 77 balls and batted for 101 minutes against South Africa in 1999 without scoring. He put on 32 in 27.2 overs with Chris Harris before getting out for 0, the longest duck in Test history. Godfrey Evans, widely regarded as England's best post-War wicket-keeper, once batted 133 minutes for 10 not out against Australia on the 1946-47 tour and helped to save a Test match. It took him 97 minutes to get off the mark, the pre-Allott record. Evans must have exercised a great deal of self-control, as he was usually a hard-hitting batsman and one of the fastest scorers around.

Yet those are trifling two-hour efforts compared to Shoaib Mohammad of Pakistan who once batted for 12 hours to score 163, and Brendon Kuruppu of Sri Lanka who batted almost 13 hours to score 201 not out. Mind you, that was three hours less than the 337 that Hanif Mohammad of Pakistan ground out in just over 16 hours. Even they seem recklessly irresponsible compared to the glacial progress of Tom Walker of Hambledon (1761-1831). In the days of underarm bowling, he faced 170 deliveries from David Harris, probably the best bowler of his era, and scored 1 run.

THE DAY SIR DONALD LET HIS HAIR DOWN

The great Sir Don Bradman preferred hitting fours to sixes, reasoning that you couldn't be caught if you kept the ball on the ground. However, on one occasion he waived this rule and hit possibly the fastest hundred ever scored.

In November 1931, already a Test player, he was invited to guest for Blackheath, New South Wales, who were playing Lithgow to celebrate the installation of a new artificial wicket. This being a festive occasion, Bradman decided to let his hair down. The highlight of his innings was the three (8-ball) over spell when he hit Lithgow for 33, 40 and 27, making a total of 100 in 22 balls. His partner faced the other two balls and scored 2, no doubt trying to get Bradman back on strike. In all he scored 256 including 14 sixes and 29 fours.

Even if neither Blackheath nor Lithgow played at the highest level,

they took their cricket seriously enough and some of their players had gone on to higher grades. The Mayor of Blackheath asked if Bradman would give them the bat as a memento. 'When I've finished with it,' Bradman replied. He split it whilst batting a couple of months later and sent it to the Mayor, having scored another five hundreds in the interim in Tests and other games, very likely using the same bat. Bearing in mind that 22 balls is substantially faster than Shahid Afridi's 37-ball record ODI effort in 1996, there is no doubt that Bradman would have coped in the limited overs era of cricket.

83 per cent of the total
Batsmen who did it on their own

Sometimes an innings completely collapses, except for one batsman who copes very effectively with the bowling and the conditions. When this happens, the statistics can throw up some extreme performances and a player can score a huge percentage of his team's total. Without delving too far into the decimal points, here are a few examples.

In 1977, the great New Zealand opening batsman Glenn Turner opened the batting for Worcestershire against Glamorgan at Swansea, after Glamorgan had batted first and made 309 for four (innings closed after 100 overs). Apart from Turner, Worcester batted poorly and were all out for 169. Turner's contribution was remarkable: he batted through the innings and made 141 not out, the next highest score being Gifford with 7. Turner's score was 83 per cent of his side's total, the highest percentage of a completed innings by a player in any first-class game.

Turner ended up with many achievements in his career. He scored over 100 centuries, the only non-English batsman other than Bradman to do so. As part of the New Zealand touring party in England in 1973, he had scored 1,000 runs by the end of May, at that time only the seventh batsman to do so and the eighth occasion this had happened (Bradman, of course, did it twice).

In 1932, the India touring team travelled to Harrogate to play

Yorkshire. The first two innings finished with only 1 run separating the two sides, but when the Indians batted again they were all out for 66 with the Yorkshire spin bowler, George Macaulay, taking his best figures of eight for 21. However, the game is memorable statistically because the India number five, Nazir Ali, scored 52 of his side's total – almost 79 per cent. The next highest contribution by a batsman was 3, although extras contributed 5.

Making a high percentage of a small total is impressive, but when a much larger total and longer innings is involved, stamina and concentration of a different order is required. The New Zealand batsman Bert Sutcliffe is perhaps the outstanding example. When Canterbury played Otago in 1952, Canterbury's first innings total of 309 was dwarfed by Sutcliffe's 385 out of his Otago team's total of 500. The next highest score was 29, made jointly by Gilbertson and by extras, an extraordinary disparity. Sutcliffe's innings represented 77 per cent of his team's total and he batted for well over seven hours, hit 46 fours and three sixes. These figures make you blink. More importantly it was a match-winning innings: Canterbury made only 98 in their second innings and lost by an innings.

Another huge contribution to a large total was made by the Namibian cricketer, Gerrie Snyman. He has played much of his cricket in the

Birmingham League and has taken part in relatively few first-class games. One exception was a match between Namibia and Kenya held in 2008, part of the ICC Intercontinental Cup that enables countries outside the Test-playing nations to play first-class cricket. Namibia batted first but trailed on the first innings by 46. All that changed in the second innings: Snyman, batting at number four, hit 230 off 201 balls, including 11 sixes and 22 fours. When he was last out, he had made 81 per cent of Namibia's total of 282. They went on to win the match by 101 runs and reach the final where they lost to Ireland.

Snyman has another remarkable innings to his credit. In a 50-over ICC World Cricket League Division Two game against United Arab Emirates in South Africa in November 2007, Namibia batted first and Snyman hit a blistering 196 off 113 balls including a world record 17 sixes. Namibia's 358 looked a formidable score but UAE knocked them in a canter with 27 balls in hand. Snyman got a taste of his own medicine, being hit for 74 off 9.3 overs.

In Test matches, the Australian Charles Bannerman leads the figures with an unbeaten 165 out of 245 against England in 1877; this was the very first Test. Bannerman's firsts in this game included the distinction of facing the first ball ever bowled in Test cricket, and of scoring the first Test century. One surprise is that Bradman ranks no higher than 24 on the list.

ONE-TEST WONDER WITH A DIFFERENCE

When he died in 1983 aged almost 91, he was England's oldest surviving Test cricketer and had held one of Test cricket's strangest and least coveted records since 1924.

Jack MacBryan was a fine all-round sportsman who won a gold medal for hockey in the 1920 Olympics. Although his first-class cricket career had started in 1911, his most productive years were 1923 and 1924 when he was selected for Test trials. Finally, aged 32, his chance came in July 1924 in the fourth Test against South Africa. The regular England number three, Jack Hearne, was injured so MacBryan replaced

him in a strong side containing the likes of Herbert Sutcliffe, Frank Woolley and Patsy Hendren.

Unfortunately for MacBryan, the match took place at Old Trafford, which lived up to its reputation for wet weather. South Africa batted first but only 66 overs were bowled on the first day and no play at all was possible on days two and three. As they were then three-day Tests, poor MacBryan never had a chance to show what he could do. By the time of the fifth Test, Hearne had recovered and MacBryan was never again selected. He was a one-Test wonder with a difference and still holds the unwanted record he took to his grave as the only Test cricketer never to have batted, bowled or dismissed anyone in the field.

The King of cricket

The Yank who struck out Ranji

'If I had been given the selection of a World Team in the years that I knew him, 1906-10,' wrote the former Australian Test player 'Ranji' Hordern in 1932, 'he would have been almost my first choice, which is wonderful considering the galaxy of players at that time (this was the Golden Age of cricket).' Indeed a former England captain, P.F. Warner, when asked who was the greatest bowler ever, also named him: 'At the top of his power and speed [he] was at least the equal of the greatest of them all.'

Were Hordern and Warner referring to one of the immortals of the period such as Victor Trumper, Ranjitsinhji, C.B. Fry, Wilfred Rhodes, Jack Hobbs or Sidney Barnes? Very surprisingly, they were championing someone who did not come from one of the traditional cricket-playing countries and who is perhaps not as widely known as he might be: the US player, John Barton 'Bart' King (1873-1965).

King's skill – unique at the time –

was the ability to swing the ball while bowling at high speed, something earlier fast bowlers had been unable to do. The Philadelphia-born King had experience as a baseball pitcher and he introduced tricks he had learned in that game when he turned to cricket. One of these was to clasp the ball above his head in both hands, like a pitcher, in the final strides of his run up, before delivering it in a perfectly orthodox fashion. His main ball was an outswinger, but he varied it with his most dangerous delivery, an inswinger that he called 'the angler'.

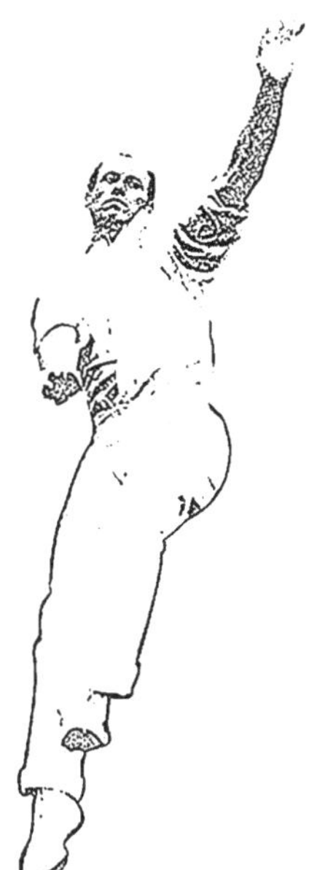

In his career – admittedly much of which was not played at first-class level – King scored almost 20,000 runs and took over 2,000 wickets. In the USA he played for teams in and around Philadelphia and won the USA's annual bowling cup on more than one occasion. In 1893, he was a member of the Gentleman of Philadelphia side playing against a full strength Australian team. In the tourists' first innings, King took four of the first five wickets to fall, ending with figures of five for 78. In a sensational result, the US team beat the visitors by an innings and 68 runs.

Yet King's reputation really rests on three tours of England where he took a large number of wickets at a very good average. Many of the country's top batsmen found him nearly unplayable. On the first tour in 1897, he took seven for 13 in the first innings against Sussex, including bowling Ranji on the first ball. King and his opening partner, E.M. Cregar, bowled unchanged and dismissed Sussex for 46 in less than an hour. In the second innings he took six for 102, as the Gentlemen of Philadelphia won by eight wickets. He batted well, too, scoring 58 in Philadelphia's first innings. In the US he once scored 344 not out, a record that still stands. Counties subsequently queued up, keen to sign him; one even offered him marriage to a rich widow as an inducement, although King wasn't interested.

On the second tour of England in 1903, highlights included scoring 98 in Philadelphia's first innings against Surrey before being run out, and 113 not out in the second, as well as taking six wickets in the match. Surrey were beaten by 110 runs and King became so exhausted he fell asleep during a speech by the Lord Chief Justice at the after-match banquet. On his third tour in 1908, he easily topped the English bowling averages by taking 87 wickets in only ten matches at 11.01. This remained the best figures for an English season until 1958. He and Hordern shared all 20 wickets in a game against South Wales.

In a career of only 65 first-class matches, he took five wickets in an innings an amazing 38 times, and ten wickets in a match on 11 occasions. He took ten wickets in an innings once and nine wickets twice. In 1912, aged 39, he was still good enough to take nine for 78 against the Australians in Philadelphia.

John Lester, one of King's teammates on the three tours, recorded one or two entertaining but apocryphal-sounding stories about him. Apparently, in a game in 1901 in Philadelphia between Belmont and Trenton, King, playing for Belmont, took the first nine wickets to fall. It is said that he then dismissed all the fielders save the one who was placed on the leg side. His job was merely to retrieve the ball and return it to the umpires when, as duly happened, King bowled the last batsman.

If King had played for England or Australia, who knows what he might have achieved? He lived to the great age of 91 and was still following cricket towards the end of his life in the US. In 1962 he received belated recognition when the MCC elected him an honorary life member.

ALL IN THE FAMILY

It is not unusual for cricketing talent to run in the family. Fourteen members of the Grace family played first-class cricket and three of them – the brothers W.G., E.M. and Fred – played for England. Seven brothers from the Foster family played for Worcestershire between 1899 and 1925 so that the county became jocularly known as Fostershire. The most famous, R.E. Foster, is the only man to have captained England at both cricket and football. He scored 287, a world record, on his Test debut. The seven Walker brothers of Southgate were also very accomplished players, four of them playing for the United All-England XI in the days before Test cricket.

Sometimes a family had enough players to make up a viable team. Generations of the Robinson family of Bristol did so every year on August Bank Holiday from 1878 to 1964, except during the War years. They played 163 times as a family unit,

winning 64, losing 71 and drawing 24. Two of the family captained Gloucestershire and one played once for England. Their most famous opponents were the Grace family whom they played at the County Ground, Bristol, in 1891, losing by 37 runs.

The ten Christopherson brothers and their father often used to play as a team in the 1870s and 1880s. One of them, Stanley, went on to play for England and was president of the MCC during the Second World War. In the early nineteenth century, the Caesar family made up a team, which played against an All-England XI. In the immediate post-Civil War period, the Newhall family of Pennsylvania also had enough members to make up a team.

Australia's Old Trafford nightmare

Jim Laker's unbeatable achievement

Unlike diamonds, cricket records are not forever. No matter how outstanding a particular feat, sooner or later someone may come along to surpass it – with one possible exception. Taking 19 out of 20 wickets in a Test match must be as close to the ultimate bowling performance as is possible. So it is hard to see anyone ever bettering Jim Laker's achievement in the fourth Ashes Test against Australia at Old Trafford in July 1956.

Although the Australians had players of the calibre of Harvey, Miller, Benaud and Lindwall, Laker's off spin bamboozled them all summer. He played seven times against them and took the huge number of 63 wickets. By the time the fourth Test match arrived, he had already taken all ten wickets in the first innings of the Surrey v. Australia game in May. He and his spin partner, the left-arm Tony Lock, took 19 of the 20 Australian wickets to fall in that match, the other being run out. They were to go one better in the Test.

Already psychologically on the back foot when they arrived at Old Trafford, Australian players complained that it was a hometown pitch, doctored for England's spinners. 'This game will be over in two days,' Keith Miller said. However, to get the most advantage from a 'hometown' wicket you need to win the toss, and that is not pre-determined. Yet England did win the toss, batted and, on a wicket that was never easy, scored a very competitive 459.

When Australia batted, England turned to spin very quickly. In just over 40 overs, Laker and Lock bowled Australia out for 84. The last seven wickets fell to Laker for 8 runs in 22 balls. He finished with nine wickets, Lock with one. The Australians were at a total loss and poked and jabbed feebly at Laker's classic bowling, only two of them reaching double figures. Their second innings was slightly more extended, but they were all out for 205 late on the last afternoon, England winning by an innings and 170 runs.

A lot of time was lost to rain and, if Australia had batted only a little better, they could have saved the game and the Ashes. Laker had taken nine for 37 in the first innings and all ten for 53 in the second, match figures of 19 for 90 – the best Test bowling performance either before, since and, very likely, ever. It is a measure of that achievement that great bowlers like Lock, Bailey and Statham, who bowled a combined total of more than 100 overs, took only one wicket between them.

This took place well before the era of high fives and celebratory bouncy huddles in the outfield. Laker was congratulated with a handshake and one or two slaps on the shoulder in a very British 'well done, old chap' sort of way. After some interviews he drove back to London, stopping off in a Lichfield pub for a drink. Laker said later that, as he was sitting at the bar, television news showed some footage of his performance, but no one in the pub associated the quiet man enjoying a pie and a pint at the counter with that amazing performance. He pressed on home arriving after 2 o'clock in the morning. After a little sleep, he set off for the Oval, as he was due to play for Surrey against – who else? – the Australians, again! The rain-curtailed game ended in a draw but he still took another five wickets.

Two bowlers sharing all 20 wickets in a Test match is extremely rare. In over 2,000 games it has happened only six times. Lock and Laker's was the fourth occasion, but it was to happen again quite soon. Less than three months later in Karachi, the Pakistani bowlers Fazal Mahmood and Khan Mohammad took all 20 wickets to earn victory in a one-off Test match. The team they were playing must have been growing used to the experience: it was the Australians and the side contained nine of the side that had been 'Lakered' at Old Trafford.

SKIRTING AROUND THE OVERARM ISSUE

The introduction of overarm bowling is one of the great turning points in the history of the game. From the dawn of cricket, all bowling was underarm. For a long time the ball was rolled along the ground similarly to bowls, and to make it easier to hit, bats were curved in the manner of hockey sticks. Then, bit by bit, the ball began to be pitched, but still underarm, and by the end of the eighteenth century bats had adjusted and become straight.

At about the same time Tom Walker (1762–1831), a famous Hampshire player, is reported to have spent his winters practising a new-fangled sort of bowling, where the arm was raised and the ball delivered at about waist height – think Malinga the Slinger, but a good deal slower. However this innovation was not acceptable to the Hambledon Club and Walker never used it in a game.

A couple of decades later, so the story goes, a young woman called Christina Willes was bowling underarm in the garden to her brother John, a well known Kent cricketer, to give him some batting practise. Her hooped skirts impeded her arm movement so she raised it higher. Willes liked the innovation and began to champion it although the authorities formally forbade it. On 15 July 1822, he did the cricketing equivalent of storming the Bastille and bowled a roundarm ball at Lord's, playing for Kent against the

MCC. On being no-balled, a report of the time says that 'he threw down the ball in high dudgeon, left the ground immediately, and (it is said) never played again.'

Yet roundarm, and then overarm, bowling was an idea whose time had arrived. Roundarm was legalised in 1835 and overarm in 1864. Underarm still remained legal and was occasionally used (see When underarm was underhand); now it is not permitted unless the captains agree. Indeed, the inscription on John Willes' tombstone at Sutton Valence reads 'He was a patron of all manly sports, and the first to introduce roundarm bowling.'

Alletson's innings

A once-in-a-lifetime knock

It is amazing how 90 minutes of batting mayhem can transform an average cricketer into an immortal. By the third day of the county match between Sussex and Nottinghamshire at Hove in 1911, the game was clearly in Sussex's hands. Notts had batted first and scored 238; Essex had replied with 414. In their second innings Notts had scored 185 – only 9 runs ahead – when their seventh wicket fell, leaving them facing a substantial defeat.

Next man in was Ted Alletson: he was primarily a fairly average fast bowler but, as his place in the batting order showed, he was not much rated as a batsman. Alletson played steadily until lunch when he was 47 and Notts had reached 260. They were 84 ahead but with only one wicket left. It was basically a lost cause and, before going out for the afternoon session, Alletson asked the Notts captain, A.O. Jones, for instructions. 'I don't think it matters what you do,' Jones said. 'Then I am going to give Tim Killick [the Sussex spinner who had taken five wickets in the first innings] some stick,' Alletson replied.

Which he duly did: in 50 balls, including 12 dot balls, he scored 142 runs, consisting of eight sixes, 18 fours, two threes, six twos and four singles. One over from Killick (which included two no-balls) went for 4, 6, 6, 0, 4, 4, 4, 6, comprising a world record 34 which survived until Gary Sobers' six maximums in 1968. According to estimates, Notts scored 142 in 40 minutes. At one stage they scored 100 in five overs, of which Alletson scored 97. When he was out on 189 to a disputed catch on the boundary, it was the end of one of the most famous innings ever played.

Sussex were left to score 237 to win; Nottingham bowled 81 overs and Sussex crept to 213 for eight when the game finished as a draw. It is worth mentioning that Alletson had an injured wrist and wasn't due to play but had to cover for someone even more incapacitated. The Sussex captain generously called it the best innings he ever saw. Subsequently Alletson played other aggressive innings but never got near to making another century.

By May 1914 his career was over.

To give some context to Alletson's achievement, it is worth looking at a couple of innings by one of the outstanding hitters of the modern day, Graham Napier of Essex. Interestingly he, like Alletson, was not primarily a batsman. Napier has twice hit 16 sixes in an innings – once in a county game against Surrey, and once in a Twenty20 game. Against Surrey, after reaching 83, he scored the next 113 in only 33 balls. He was out on 196, going for the six that would have given him both a double century and the world record number of sixes. His Twenty20 innings of 152 not out against Sussex was scored off only 58 balls. Such power hitting, plus his good-quality fast-medium bowling, seemed to make him a natural for

England's Twenty20 squad. However he had come on the scene a bit late in the day and was troubled by injuries; an international career never quite clicked for him.

So, Alletson or Napier? Their eras are 100 years apart and comparisons are invidious. We should leave each with their outstanding individual achievements.

THE WIFE WHO CAME A PURLER

When Roy Park was chosen to make his Test debut for Australia in the second 1920–21 Ashes Test at Melbourne, it was naturally a very proud occasion and his wife went along to support him. Possibly she wasn't particularly interested in cricket, because she took along her knitting to help pass the time while waiting for her husband's big moment.

This came (and went) quite soon. Australia batted first and with the score at 116 the first wicket fell. At number three, Park strode out to face the England opening bowler, Howell. He suffered every Test debutant's nightmare and was bowled first ball. Up in the stands his wife had applauded him out to the wicket, but had dropped her knitting needle while he was taking guard and bent down to retrieve it. By the time she was ready to re-focus on the cricket, her husband was already on the way back to the pavilion. Park did not have a chance to redeem himself as Australia won by an innings. He was never selected for Australia again, so his wife had missed his entire Test career.

Park's failure had mitigating circumstances but it was not until years later that he told his son-in-law the whole story. Park was a qualified doctor and had been called out the night before the game to attend a birth. Due to difficulties with the delivery he had stayed all night and hadn't got to bed. His son-in-law was in a good position to understand,

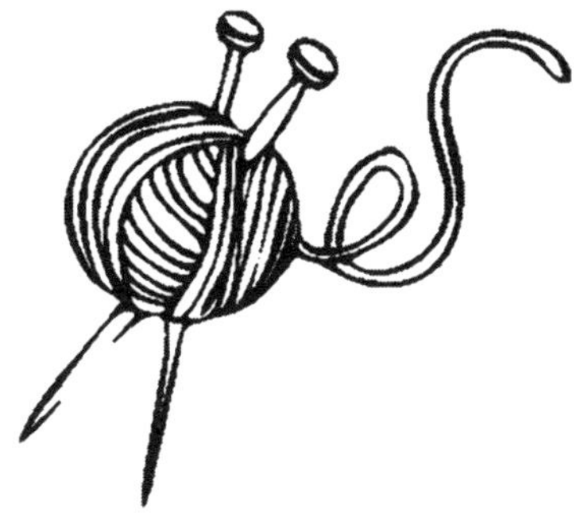

being Ian Johnson who captained Australia against England in the 1950s. He said of his father-in-law that he always placed his patient's welfare first and never made excuses.

Struck out of sight
Off-days of the great bowlers

ODIs are no respecters of reputations. A list of the best bowlers in the world in recent years would certainly include Muttiah Muralitharan and Lasith Malinga (Sri Lanka), Steve Harmison and Jimmy Anderson (England), Dale Steyn (South Africa) and Waqar Younis (Pakistan). But these famous names are also near the top of another list that they would prefer you not to mention – the list of most runs conceded in an ODI innings. Look away now if you can't stand the sight of blood.

The off spinner Muttiah Muralitharan is the record holder for most wickets in both Test (800) and one-day cricket (534), so he knows how to bowl, yet on 12 February 2006 the Australians walloped him for 99 in ten overs. In 2004, Steve Harmison bowled fearsomely fast against the West Indies and topped the Test match rankings for bowlers; yet in July 2006, Sri Lanka battered him for 97 off ten overs. Jimmy Anderson, one of England's most successful fast bowlers of recent years, has had several visits to this list with analyses of one for 91 (twice) and one for 86. Dale Steyn, regarded as the fastest bowler of his

day, took none for 89 off ten overs against India in February 2010 – at this time he was the highest-ranked bowler in Test cricket. Waqar Younis was one of the outstanding fast bowlers of his generation with 373 Test and 416 ODI wickets; however, playing against Sri Lanka in 1998, he took two for 86.

Perhaps the most surprising name to appear on this list is that of Malinga the Slinger, possibly the most effective 'death' bowler in limited overs cricket. His fearsome, toe-crushing, in-swinging yorkers made him extremely hard to score off. However this was not the case on 28 February 2012. With India needing a very unlikely 321 in 40 overs to remain in the Commonwealth Bank Series, Kohli, the India number four, made mincemeat of the target. He glanced Malinga with delicate timing first to one side of fine leg, then the other, hitting him for 24 off one over. Kohli scored 133 not out from 86 deliveries, his last 83 coming off 42 balls. Malinga was hit for 96 off 7.4 overs. Giving up 12.52 runs per over makes him the most expensive bowler in the history of ODIs.

A mention should also be given to four not quite so well-known bowlers who have conceded more than 100 runs off their ration of ODI overs: Brian Vitori (Zimbabwe), Tim Southee and Martin Snedden (New Zealand) have all conceded 105. But comfortably topping the list is Mick Lewis (Australia) with 113 off ten overs (*see* The greatest ODI ever?). It is perhaps not too surprising to learn that he never played for Australia again.

LINDSAY IN A SPIN

Lindsay Kline, the Australian Test spinner who played from 1955 to 1962, was bowling for Victoria against South Australia in the Sheffield Shield when he happened to kick off the bails as he bowled. The ball was hit down to third man but due to a mix up in the running, both batsmen ended up at the striker's end. The ball was quickly returned to the bowler's end, giving an excellent chance for a run out.

However, Kline couldn't remove the bails – he had already kicked them off. If he had simply replaced one of the bails and then removed it, one of

the batsmen would have been run out. But this can be a bit fiddly and is not nearly as well known as the usual practice, which is for the fielder to pull a stump from the ground whilst holding the ball against it.

Under pressure, Kline had a mental blackout. He dimly remembered that he had to pull one of the stumps out of the ground so he did, and let it drop to the ground. He also knew that at some stage he should put the ball against the stump, so he placed the ball against the stump on the ground and appealed heartily. 'Not out!' responded the umpire correctly. Not able to figure out what he had done wrong, Kline pulled out the second and then the third stump and placed the ball against them in the same way. 'Not out!' repeated the umpire.

Now all three stumps were lying on the ground. Few options remained, but the one Kline came up with left everyone in hysterics: he got down on his hands and knees and started rubbing the ball in the stump holes.

The greatest ODI ever?

The game that broke six records

There has always been plenty of rivalry and good cricket played between South Africa and Australia. The five-match ODI series in South Africa in 2005-06 was no exception. South Africa took a 2-0 lead before Australia won game three and then levelled the score after a very tense fourth game in Durban, which they won by one wicket in the last over.

So the fifth and final game in Johannesburg was the decider and at the interval there was only one team in it. Australia had amassed the record-breaking ODI total of 434 for four in their 50 overs; Ricky Ponting, the Australian captain, had hit 164 off 105 balls, still his highest ODI score. The South Africans' bowling was a shambles: Makhaya Ntini had gone for 80 runs off nine overs and Jacques Kallis, a world-class all-rounder, for 70 off six overs.

The previous best team score – 398 for five by Sri Lanka in 1996 against one of the minnows, Kenya – was easily eclipsed by Australia. No one gave South Africa a chance; teams chasing large totals usually crumbled under the pressure. The best reply so far had been Pakistan's 344 for eight in 2004, chasing 349 against India. They had got within 5 runs, but even that score was 91 runs less than South Africa required. History said it just wasn't on.

South Africa needed to score at a rate of 8.7 runs an over, or two fours an over with a single on top. According to Mike Selvey of *The Guardian*, in the interval the South African A.B. de Villiers is reported to have remarked drily to his teammates, 'The bowlers have done their job, now it's the batsmen's turn.'

The key to South Africa's reply would be the response of their early order batsmen, in particular Graeme Smith, the captain, and Herschelle Gibbs. They came together after an early wicket fell and both were inspired. Together they put on 187 in 20.5 overs at almost 9 runs an over. The momentum was maintained throughout the innings but wickets were falling.

However, at the start of the last over, South Africa at 428 for eight needed just 7 with Boucher and Hall,

two experienced lower-order players, at the crease. They seemed to have things under control, although all results were still possible, especially with only the unpredictable Makhaya Ntini to come in at number 11. It was a dramatic final over: after a single and a four bit off most of the required 7, Andrew Hall tried to finish it in one shot and was caught.

Suddenly, Ntini, whom you would not have wanted to bat for your life, was facing the rapid Brett Lee and Australia were back in it. Somehow or other, Ntini got some bat on the fourth ball and squeezed it down to third man for single. The scores were tied with two balls left for Boucher to win it. One was enough, as he hit Lee to the boundary.

With South Africa winning by one wicket off the penultimate ball in such a high-scoring game amid scenes of great excitement, it was always likely that the press would dub it 'the greatest game'. Yet others, such as the brilliant former South African batsman Barry Richards, begged to differ and thought such high scores were bad for the game and detrimental to bowlers.

The Australian fast bowler Mick Lewis would probably have agreed. He had played in two of the four previous games and had not performed too badly. However, the sky fell in on him in this game. He gave away 113 runs in his ten overs, the worst one-day analysis ever recorded. Jacque Kallis leaked runs at a greater rate than Lewis, but his captain had mercy and took him off, so he didn't get to bowl the full ten. Otherwise, the unwanted place at the top of the list might have been his and not Lewis's.

The game was one of records. No other has come close to the aggregate number of runs of 872. The total of 26 sixes and 89 fours were the most in a game up to that point as, in turn, was each side's score. Yet possibly the most amazing feature is that South Africa actually thought they could win the game – and did. Their new record total didn't last long. Later that year, Sri Lanka scored 443 for nine against the less demanding opposition of the Netherlands.

THE CHIEF WHO TOOK UMBRAGE

W.G. Grace and Sir Donald Bradman, kings of cricket in their day, had their well-documented autocratic moments. Grace would sometimes refuse to leave the crease when out and Bradman earned the nickname 'The Don of Dons' for his absolute control of Australian cricket. Both, however, might have learnt something from Ratu Lala, the High Chief of Taveuni, one of the largest islands in Fiji.

Cricket has been played in Fiji since the 1870s and in the early days, the authority of the High Chiefs of the larger islands was paramount. For example, a toss was unnecessary as the Chief's team could bat first as a given right. The batting order was hierarchical and the High Chief would usually open the innings

himself. While he was batting, the opposing captain could not change the bowling without asking his permission 'in a crouching posture of respect' in the middle of the pitch. Of course if the Chief was enjoying the bowling, he was unlikely to agree.

In a game against the province of Bau in 1908, Ratu Lala opened the batting and received the customary trial ball. His own islanders always gave him a few easy runs in deference to his semi-divine status but the Bau team was not so respectful: the chief was out bowled first ball. Seriously offended by this* lèse majesté *he grabbed the stumps and stalked off, ordering his followers to leave. The game had lasted only one ball but the effects lasted 20 years, the length of time Ratu Lala banned the playing of cricket in Taveuni.

Through the covers
Cricket and the literary link

There have always been strong associations between cricket and literature. C.B. Fry (1872-1956) played cricket and football at international level, as well as excelling in other sports. As the editor and publisher of magazines, he developed a wide circle of literary acquaintances, which included J. M. Barrie, who wrote Peter Pan, John Galsworthy, author of *The Forsyte Saga*, and Ben Travers, the writer of *Rookery Nook* and many other farces. Fry also knew Sir Arthur Conan Doyle, the creator of Sherlock Holmes, who had actually played first-class cricket. Because of his cricketing exploits, Fry was something of a hero to these distinguished writers; he used to complain that whenever he wanted to discuss literature with them, all they wanted to talk about was cricket.

P.G. Woodhouse played for his school first eleven and remained so smitten by cricket throughout his life that his most famous character Jeeves, who first appeared in 1915, was named after a Warwickshire cricketer,

Percy Jeeves. Wodehouse saw Jeeves play in 1913 and was impressed by his neatness and bearing. Considered a cricketer with great promise, Jeeves died in 1916, aged 20, in the trenches during the First World War.

Samuel Beckett, author of *Waiting for Godot* and other plays, is the only Nobel Laureate with an obituary in *Wisden*; he is also the only Nobel Laureate to have played first-class cricket. He played two games for Dublin University against Northamptonshire in 1925 and 1926, although without much distinction, scoring 35 runs in four innings and bowling 23 overs without taking a wicket. Whether that disappointing experience contributed to his somewhat bleak view of life is not known.

The Nobel playwright Harold Pinter was a lifelong devotee of cricket. He played regularly at club level and wrote a memoir of the Somerset and England cricketer, Arthur Wellard. In his play *No Man's Land*, four main characters – Hirst, Spooner, Briggs and Foster – are named after first-class cricketers of the late nineteenth and early twentieth centuries.

The novelist John Fowles, whose work included *The French Lieutenant's Woman* and *The Magus*, was a promising schoolboy cricketer, good enough to have had a trial for Essex.

Of the many books written about cricket, one of the most unusual is *A La Recherche du Cricket Perdu* by Simon Barnes, currently the Chief Sports Writer of *The Times*. The book includes 'previously unpublished' extracts from works by Shakespeare (*The Tragedy of Prince*

Botham Part Two), Samuel Pepys (*The Oval Diaries*), Oscar Wilde (*The Importance of Being Captain*), D.H. Lawrence (*The Virgin and the All-Rounder*) and Ian Fleming, author of the James Bond novels, (*You're Only Out Once*), amongst others.

In 1907, a team of Authors fancied themselves sufficiently to challenge a team of Actors to a game. With Sir Arthur Conan Doyle, P.G. Wodehouse, A.A. Milne and E.W. Hornung of Raffles fame on the Authors' side they had a distinguished line-up, if you were stocking a library. In fact they were well and truly hammered by the Actors who unfairly fielded C. Aubrey Smith, a former England captain (*see* From sightscreen to silver screen), and Basil Foster, one of the famous Worcestershire cricket family and a current first-class cricketer.

RECORDS GALORE FOR 13-YEAR-OLDS

In November 2006, two 13-year-olds went out to open the batting for St Peter's High School, Hyderabad, India, in a game against St Philip's High School. By the time the innings came to a close 40 overs later, Manoj Kumar had scored 320 and Shaibaz Tumbi 324, both not out, and the pair had put on 721, a world record stand for any wicket in any form of cricket. The boys were naturally thrilled to have beaten the previous record of 664, also set in a schools' game, particularly as it had been established by two players who went on to become Test cricketers.

One of the pair was Sachin Tendulkar who became one of the icons of the modern cricketing era, scoring the highest number of Test runs and making over 50 centuries at an average of over 55. The other was Vinod Kambli, who had a more chequered career. He started with immense promise, scoring four centuries, including two double centuries, in his first seven Test innings. However the bowlers worked

him out, and other factors – including indiscipline – came into play. Kambli also became obsessed by the width of his bat handle, sometimes batting with as many as nine grips, probably also a world record. Eventually he was dropped from both Test and one-day sides.

Two other records were set in the Hyderabad schoolboy game. The score of 721 is the highest total in any form of limited over cricket. And when St Peter's bowled out their dispirited opponents for only 21, the winning margin of 700 was the highest in any game. The lads have ambitions to play Test cricket and it will be interesting to see if they follow in the footsteps of their great idol, Sachin Tendulkar.

The longest gap
22 years between matches

John Traicos is one of the very few cricketers to have played Test cricket for more than one country. He is also unique in that he was born in one country but played in Test matches for two others. Born in 1947 of Greek ancestry in Zagazig, Egypt, the following year Traicos migrated with his family to Southern Rhodesia, which became Zimbabwe in 1980. The twists and turns of international and cricket politics in the period from 1970 to 1992 certainly affected his career and resulted in him setting one amazing record that will probably never be beaten.

Traicos began to play cricket seriously at Natal University and was coached by the great South African all-rounder, Trevor Goddard. He made such progress that in 1970, aged only 22, he was selected to play for South Africa as an off spinner in the three-Test series against Australia. He says of his performance that it was only 'average'. Immediately after the series, the Test careers of himself and his teammates, including Goddard,

Barry Richards, Eddie Barlow, and Graham and Peter Pollock, came to a grinding halt when South Africa was banned from Test cricket because of its apartheid policy, a ban which was to last until 1991.

In the meantime, Zimbabwe had begun to play international cricket at one-day level, including a famous 13 run victory over Australia in the 1983 World Cup, a game in which Traicos played for the African side. Eventually Zimbabwe was awarded Test status: an Inaugural Test was arranged to take place in October 1992 in Harare against India, whose team included Kapil Dev, Tendulkar, Azharuddin and many other household names. Traicos, aged 45, was selected for Zimbabwe; this match would take place exactly 22 years and 222 days after his last Test appearance.

It is substantially the longest gap between Test appearances in cricket history. Alistair Campbell, one of his new teammates, had not even been born when Traicos had last played Test cricket. Meanwhile in April 1992, South Africa had played its first Test since the ban was lifted. Of all those who had played in the last pre-ban match in 1970, only Traicos had bridged the gap to the new era, in the process becoming the 12th oldest person to play Test cricket.

Zimbabwe drew the match but Traicos's performance was far from average this time as he recorded his best Test bowling figures of five for 86, his victims including Tendulkar, Azharruddin and Kapil Dev. The final turn of the political wheel came in 1997, when he moved to Australia as a result of political instability in Zimbabwe.

THE RECORD THAT *WISDEN* IGNORED

A **Wisden** *obituary usually leaps on any unique quality that helps to provide some colour and interest to the life of the deceased cricketer. However it conspicuously failed to do so in the case of the Jamaica and West Indies cricketer, Leslie Hylton. 'Hylton,' the notice began, 'died in Jamaica on May 17, 1955, aged 50.' It went on to say that he was a fast bowler who had played 40 times for Jamaica and six times for the West Indies, and had been part of the 1939 touring party to England. It commented that he had met with 'moderate success',* **Wisden**-*speak for having had an awful Test series. End of obit.*

Wisden *was too shy to note that Hylton was probably as unique as a cricketer can get: he is the only Test cricketer known to have been executed for murder. His wife Lurline had been away in New York and Hylton received an anonymous letter saying that she was living with another man. Having ordered her home, he subsequently shot her – under provocation, he was later to plead.*

The trial took place in 1954 and Noel Nethersole, who had been his Jamaica team captain, defended Hylton in court. The following year Nethersole became Minister of Finance yet, despite his presence, the jury did not accept the defence of manslaughter. There was evidence that Hylton had shot his wife seven times, meaning he had reloaded his revolver. Although the jury strongly recommended mercy, appeals were

turned down and he went to the gallows. It is curious that from time to time* Wisden *has felt obliged to airbrush the record when it is not to the credit of cricket or of cricketers who are, after all, only human.

Cricket's greatest name?
A rival to Grace and Bradman

The cricketing reputation of John Wisden (1826-1884) has been very much overshadowed by the renown of the annual he founded – *Wisden's Cricketers' Almanack* or *Wisden* as it is always called. Yet his contemporaries regarded Wisden as possibly the best all-rounder of the time; indeed one of his bowling performances is so outstanding that it has never been matched since it happened in July 1850.

Although his batting was useful, bowling was Wisden's strong suit. He made an excellent first-class debut for Sussex against Kent in 1845, aged only 18, taking nine wickets in the match. Only a year later, he was selected for an England side that played Kent, taking four wickets.

A quickish off break bowler, his *annus mirabilis* was probably 1850 when he took 340 wickets in 38 matches across all forms of cricket. His crowning performance took place the same year for North against South at Lord's. He took three South wickets in their first innings, but in the second he took all the South wickets, amazingly clean bowling all ten batsmen, the only time this has happened in first-class cricket (*see* Jennings Tune on song). In the corresponding fixture the following year, he switched allegiance and played for South, taking ten wickets in the match. That same year, 1851, he again took all ten wickets for 58 in an innings for an England XI against Yorkshire XIV.

Wisden took over 1,100 first-class wickets in his career and his performances earned him the nickname of 'The Little Wonder', the 'little' referring to his height of 5ft 4.5in (1.5m). He retired in 1863 and founded his famous publication the following year; he died of cancer in 1884, aged 57. In 1913, 27 years after his death, he was chosen as the sole *Wisden* Cricketer of the

Year, one of only four occasions when just one cricketer has been selected (*see* Five of the best).

Fans of W.G. Grace or Sir Donald Bradman will debate whether John Wisden is a greater cricketing name than either or both of them. As a cricketer, Wisden certainly has to bow the knee to both. His lasting fame rests on the *Almanack* continuously published since 1864, which may mean that his name-recognition is greater than even those two giants. Wisden is still much appreciated in his hometown of Brighton where a bus is named after him. His spirit would no doubt be pleased if its route passes the Sussex county ground in Hove.

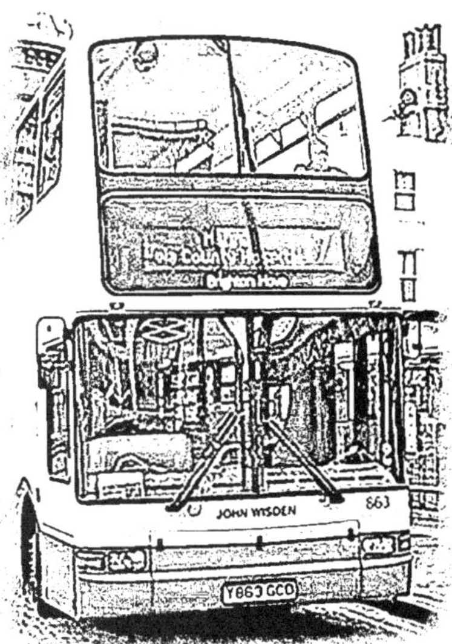

THE MOST WIDELY READ *WISDEN*

When E.W. (Jim) Swanton, one of the most respected cricket writers and commentators, was captured by the Japanese in 1942 and made a prisoner-of-war, he had on his person a 1939 copy of* Wisden *which he was allowed to retain. Cricket was a great morale booster in the camp: the prisoners organised matches and Swanton made his* Wisden *available to read. So many prisoners wanted to borrow the book that the loan period was restricted to six hours. Despite all the handling he was able to preserve it throughout the war and brought it back with him to England. Swanton later said he thought it was the most read copy of* Wisden *ever published; after his death it passed to the Lord's Museum and is on display there.

Cricket in high places…
…And low places, cold places and wet places

Jane Austen, who was familiar with cricket, might well have begun *Pride and Prejudice*, 'It is a truth universally acknowledged that a cricket lover desperate for a game will play anywhere.' Although she didn't, it is unarguably true. Show a cricketer a mountainside, a glacier or a pool-strewn foreshore, and no matter how unpromising the terrain he or she will immediately call for bat, ball and stumps.

In 1823, give or take a year, Captain William Parry's expedition to discover a Northwest Passage had to winter near the island of Igloolik at latitude 3 degrees north of the Arctic Circle. Parry encouraged the crews of HMS *Fury* and HMS *Hecla* to play cricket, football and quoits. An illustration by George Lyon, captain of the *Hecla*, shows a game of cricket in progress with a ship marooned in the distance.

At the other end of the world, in 1985 a game was played at the field-camp of the United States Antarctic Field Programme at 83.30 degrees south during the course of an international workshop. The pitch roller was probably the largest ever used: a C130 Hercules aircraft. One of the most common causes of dismissal during this game was 'retired frozen'. A tennis rather than a cricket ball was used for fear the harder ball would get lost in the snow. Bad light was not an issue as the sky remained bright until midnight.

In 2009, a Twenty20 game was played 16,946ft (5,165m) up Mount Everest, setting a new world altitude record for a cricket game and raising funds for charity. The site was chosen for its resemblance to the Oval according to the expedition leader, Richard Kirtley. The teams were appropriately called Hillary, which won, and Tenzing.

The Brambles sandbank in the Solent, midway between Southampton and the Isle of Wight, occasionally emerges above sea level but only for about an hour. This very short period is just enough time for the Royal Southern Yacht Club from Southampton and the Island Sailing Club from the Isle of Wight to rush out in their boats to play as much cricket as they can before the bank is again submerged, at which point everyone retires to the bar of the pre-arranged winner.

One to look forward to is a game to be played 1 mile (1.6km) underground in the Honister slate mine situated between Borrowdale and Buttermere in the Lake District. Plans for a match between the villages of Threlkeld and Braithwaite were well advanced in December 2011, but had to be put on hold at the last moment because of heavy snow.

Cricket is played in many unexpected places, ranging from Afghanistan to Zambia via China, France, Indonesia, Rwanda, Slovenia and Turkey. Perhaps it is easier to ask where it isn't played.

SELECTED BIBLIOGRAPHY

Books

Barker, Felix, *The House that Stoll Built*, Frederick Muller Ltd, 1957

Barnes, Simon, *A La Recherche du Cricket Perdu*, MacMillan London Ltd, 1989

Caffyn, William, *Seventy-One Not Out*, William Blackwood & Sons, 1900

Chalke, Stephen with Bomber Wells, *One More Run*, Fairfield Books, 2000

Chappell, Ian, Robertson, Austin and Rigby, Paul, *Chappelli has the Last Laugh*, Landsdowne Press, 1980

Dodds, Dickie, *Hit Hard and Enjoy It*, The Cricketer, 1976

Gibbs, Herschelle, *To the Point*, Zebra Press, 2010

Gibson, Alan, *Growing Up with Cricket*, William Collins, 1985

Grace, W.G. with Arthur Porritt, *Cricketing Reminiscences and Personal Recollections*, James Bowden, 1899

Griffiths, Peter and Bartlett, Kit, *John Wisden: His Record Innings-by-Innings*, Association of Cricket Statisticians and Historians, 1999

Haigh, Gideon, *Australian Cricket Anecdotes*, OUP, 1996

Haigh, Gideon, *Parachutist at Fine Leg and Other Unusual Occurrences from Wisden*, Aurum Press, 2007

Haigh, Gideon, *Peter the Lord's Cat and Other Unexpected Obituaries from Wisden*, Aurum Press, 2006

Harold, J., *The Art of Sledging*, Allen & Unwin (Australia), 2008

Hodgson, R.L, *Cricket Memories*, Methuen & Co, 1930

Horrall, Andrew, *Popular Culture in London c.1980-1918*, Manchester University Press, 2001

Lillee, Dennis, *My Life in Cricket*, Methuen Australia, 1982

Mason, Ronald, *Sing All a Green Willow*, Epworth Press, 1967

Nyren, John, *The Progress of Cricket*, republished Davis-Poynter, 1974

Rice, Jonathan, *Curiosities of Cricket*, Pavilion Books, 1993

Scott, Les, *Bats, Balls & Bails*, Bantam Press, 2009

Shaw, Alfred, *Alfred Shaw, Cricketer, His Career & Reminiscences:* recorded by A.W. Pullin, Cassell & Co, 1902

Snow, C. P., *Variety of Men*, Penguin, 1967

Snow, P.A., *Cricket in the Fiji Islands*, Whitcomb & Tombs, 1949

Waghorn, H.T., *Cricket Scores: 1730-1773*, William Blackwood, 1899

Waghorn, H.T., *The Dawn of Cricket*, R. Tomsett & Co, 1906

Ward, Andrew, *Cricket's Strangest Matches*, Robson Books, 2001

Wilde, Simon, *Ranji: The Strange Genius of Ranjitsinhji*, Aurum Press, 2003

Newspapers, journals and websites

Athens News

BBC News

Inside Sport (Australia)

The Cricketer

The Daily Mail

The Daily Telegraph

The Economist

The Guardian

The Independent

The Western Mail

CricketArchive.com

ESPN Cricinfo

From Lads to Lord's: The History of Cricket 1761–1770

Wikipedia

ABBREVIATIONS AND GLOSSARY OF SELECTED CRICKET TERMS

CHUCKER is a bowler whose action is illegal or dubious

DEATH BOWLING is a term used to describe bowling at the end of an innings in a limited overs game when the batsmen tend to hit out at everything

DOT BALL is a ball off which no run is scored

ECB is the England and Wales Cricket Board, the governing body of cricket in England and Wales

FIRST-CLASS MATCHES are games between teams of a sufficiently high standard. The game must be of two innings per side and scheduled to last at least three days, although due to circumstances this may not always happen

ICC is the International Cricket Council, the international governing body of cricket

LBW means leg before wicket, one of the ten methods of dismissal in cricket

LIST A MATCHES are broadly-speaking the equivalent of matches between first-class sides in a one-day format

MAXIMUM is a hit for six

MCC is Marylebone Cricket Club, founded in 1787. It was formerly the governing body of all cricket, a role now performed by the ICC, although the MCC acts as guardian of the rules and the spirit of the game

NO BALL is an illegitimate delivery by the bowler. A penalty run (or runs) are added to the batting team's score and the ball has to be re-bowled

ODI is a One Day International, usually matches of 50 overs per innings between countries

W.G. is an abbreviation for W.G. Grace

TWENTY20 is a form of cricket of 20 overs per side

TCCB is the Test and County Cricket Board, now superseded by the ECB

TIMELESS TEST or game means a game to be played to the finish no matter how long that takes

WISDEN in italics refers to *Wisden Cricketers' Almanack*, an annual publication frequently referred to as 'cricket's bible'. Unitalicised, **WISDEN** refers to John Wisden, founder of *Wisden Cricketers' Almanack*

INDEX

PICTURE CREDITS

The following image has been modified from the sources below and permission is granted to copy, distribute and/or modify under the terms of the GNU Free Documentation Creative Commons Attribution-ShareAlike 3.0 license; pg 33 http://en.wikipedia.org/wiki/File:Collinsplaque.jpg © Brookie

The following images have been modified from the sources below and permission is granted to copy, distribute and/or modify under the terms of the GNU Free Documentation Creative Commons Attribution-ShareAlike 2.0 Generic license; p41 http://en.wikipedia.org/wiki/File:Botham_batting_-_geograph.org.uk_-_257722.jpg © Stanley Howe http://www.geograph.org.uk/profile/7629 (source http://www.geograph.org.uk/photo/257722), pg 97 http://commons.wikimedia.org/wiki/File:Tendulkar_batting_against_Australia,_October_2010_%281%29,_cropped.jpg © Pulkit Sinha (http://www.flickr.com/photos/13320526@N05)

The following images have been modified from the sources below and permission is granted to copy, distribute and/or modify under the terms of the GNU Free Documentation Creative Commons Attribution-ShareAlike 2.5 Generic license; pg45 http://commons.wikimedia.org/wiki/File:Old_bracelets_%28aka%29.jpg © André Karwath, p116 http://commons.wikimedia.org/wiki/File:Pm_cricket_shots09_5910.jpg © Privatemusings

The following images have been modified from the sources below and permission is granted to copy, distribute and/or modify under the terms of the Creative Commons Attribution-ShareAlike 3.0 Unported license; pg 54 http://commons.wikimedia.org/wiki/File:Sobers_statue_kensington.jpg © Winton Edghill, pg 64 http://commons.wikimedia.org/wiki/File:Wes_durston_batting.jpg © Harrias, p67 http://commons.wikimedia.org/wiki/File:Muttiah_Muralitharan-web.jpg © Celidh, pg70 http://commons.wikimedia.org/wiki/File:SteveBucknor.JPG © Daniel, pg 78 http://commons.wikimedia.org/wiki/File:Herschelle_Gibbs.jpg © YellowMonkey/Blnguyen, p119 http://commons.wikimedia.org/wiki/File:Jacques_Kallis_2.jpg © YellowMonkey/Blnguyen

All other images have been modified from source images that are in the Public Domain either because the copyright has expired or the author has released it as such.

MORE AMAZING TITLES

LOVED THIS BOOK?

Tell us what you think and you could win another fantastic book from David & Charles in our monthly prize draw.

www.lovethisbook.co.uk

AMAZING & EXTRAORDINARY FACTS: JAMES BOND

Michael Paterson

ISBN: 978-1-4463-0195-1

The essential companion for every Bond fan, unearthing a selection of surprising and intruiging facts about the much-loved fictional spy, and the books and films that he has starred in. It is brimming with strange and amusing stories about the Bond actors, from Sean Connery to Daniel Craig, behind the scenes at the film set, and amazing facts about Ian Fleming's original novel.

AMAZING & EXTRAORDINARY FACTS: FOOTBALL

Anton Rippon

ISBN: 978-1-4463-0250-7

Amazing & Extraordinary Facts: Football explores some of the most bizarre football events throughout history, from its birth during the Industrial Revolution, to the major tournaments of the Beautiful Game in the 21st century.

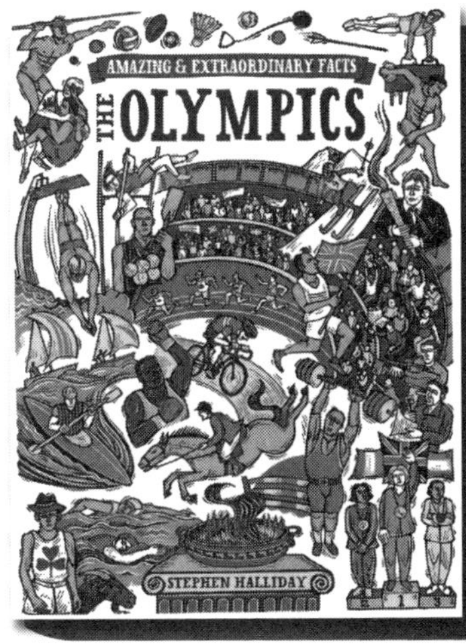

AMAZING & EXTRAORDINARY FACTS: THE OLYMPICS

Stephen Halliday

ISBN: 978-1-4463-0201-9

A unique and entertaining collection of facts surrounding the Olympic Games. From their origins in ancient Greece to the most famous Olympic medalists, the book covers a range of fascinating trivia for every sport lover to enjoy. You can discover the athletes who have set the marks for modern sporting excellence, and wonder at the records set by competitors across the years.

A DAVID & CHARLES BOOK

David & Charles is an imprint of F&W Media International, Ltd
Brunel House, Forde Close, Newton Abbot, TQ12 4PU, UK

F&W Media International, Ltd is a subsidiary of F+W Media, Inc
10151 Carver Road, Suite #200, Blue Ash, OH 45242, USA

First published in the UK in 2012

A catalogue record for this book is available from the British Library.

ISBN-13: 978-1-4463-0250-7 hardback
ISBN-10: 1-4463-0250-4 hardback

Printed in Finland by Bookwell for:
F&W Media International, Ltd
Brunel House, Forde Close, Newton Abbot, TQ12 4PU, UK

10 9 8 7 6 5 4 3 2 1

Junior Acquisitions Editor: Verity Graves-Morris
Junior Designer: Jennifer Stanley
Project Editor: Freya Dangerfield
Production Manager: Beverley Richardson